Tom,

I hope you enjoy this one
more than the first - lots
of adventures.

All the best,

Kim

Fly Baby

The Story of an American Girl

by Kimberley Jochl

Wilfred Lee Books
Village of Sugar Mountain, North Carolina
www.kimberleyjochl.com

ISBN 978-0-9971507-1-1

Cover and interior designs: Diana Wade dwadegraphics.com

Cover photography: Judy Schmidinger

TABLE OF CONTENTS

Photo credit: Todd Bush www.bushphoto.com

Also by Kimberley Jochl

The Aviatrix: Fly Like a Girl

For Gunther,
the strong and confident sunshine in every day
and the sparkling, hopeful stars and
moonlight in every night

*If you have kids who are athletically talented,
do everything you can to nurture that gift.*
—Lukas Gehrer,
Dad's neighbor and friend from Gaissau, Austria

INTRODUCTION

Blond. Blue-eyed. And female. Society's stereotypical ingredients for a dingbat. Surely I had no choice but to receive those arguably attractive, superficial traits that shape my daily life, dictate who I am, and determine my future. Oh, that's rubbish! Of course I had a choice in who I would become and where I would end up. My older sister, my twin sister, my little brother, my mom, my dad, my husband, and our daughter shaped who I am today. The disposition God programmed into my soul probably had something to do with it too.

Some have said that I'm an overachiever, or that I can do better. Some have said I'm aggressive, some that I'm charming. Some have said I'm a wimp, some that I'm too direct. Some have said I'm a follower, some that I'm always one step ahead. Some have said I'm a wingman. Some have said I'm prickly (go figure), and some have just called me a pushy little fucker.

Mom says I'm a pretty girl, and smart. But she says that to my sisters, Sherri and Krista, too. She also says I'm a good listener. Dad says I'm level-headed and responsible. Krista says I'm as beautiful as my favorite color, light blue. My husband Gunther says I'm his pebble, and that I have the prettiest smile in the whole world. Our daughter, Olivia, says every night when I put her to bed, "You're the best."

I say that action and performance speak more truthfully than the spoken or written word. And yet here I am writing a book. *What's that all about?*

In a word, a contradiction.

Well, no . . . my story is about love, cheerful and inspiring addiction, determination, failure, achievement, heartbreak, courage, discipline, fulfillment, joy, faith, sports, flying, and being a girl. Come on, I'll show you.

CHAPTER ONE
Little Girls

My identical twin sister and I love each other like crazy. For years we did everything together. We even competed around the world as members of the United States Alpine Ski Team.

You should know that twins are always very clear and quite defensive about who is the "oldest," who is the "youngest," and by exactly how many minutes. Yet Krista and I still differ on the story of how we met and how we entered the world.

Krista thinks we met two weeks after our birth. Here's what *she* says: "Kimberley is the twin sister I didn't know until my two-week birthday. I was discharged from my very plush and peaceful (albeit sterile) incubator, only to arrive home to a noisy, chubby, twin, who realized that life with me would have to be shared. I made sure it was full of escapades and mischief, something she couldn't have done without."

Yeah, right! That's Krista's version of the beginning.

Of course, she already knew me in the womb. And if my memory serves me right, Krista was scared and didn't want to leave the safety of Mom, or me for that matter. That's why I had to push her out of the womb and into the world. Ten minutes later, I rustled up enough energy to enter the world myself.

Krista was born a measly four pounds, eleven ounces. She said I took all the food. I was the healthy, happy six-pound baby. That's when I got the nickname Chub. Think about it. I'm six pounds: normal, healthy. By no means chubby. But because

Krista was a tiny, four-pound-eleven-ounce, chicken-looking creature, her nickname is Skinny. You can believe that with the nickname "Chub," I was already scarred for life within hours of my birth. That's how Mom and Dad told us apart during those first months. Even though we're grown up now, they still look to see who has the fatter, rounder face. Me, of course. Chub. Because of my size, I got the longer name: Kimberley. Krista got the shorter name.

I'm not chubby. I'm five feet five inches, 125 pounds. Sometimes 130, but whenever the scale inches that high, I cut out the ice cream and chocolate for a week or so. I am not chubby—just my face.

Mom and Dad took me home to our cozy gingerbread house on the east side of Laurel Street in Lee, Massachusetts. Krista was left at the hospital in the incubator, so she could fatten up. I loved my new digs: spacious, quiet, loads of attention, and lots of love from Mom, Dad, and Sherri, my six-year-old sister. (Erich, my baby brother, joined us five years later.) It was ALL me. More than once I heard Mom and Dad tell people that I was the best baby when I arrived home from the hospital: I never cried and was a pleasant and wonderfully tempered baby girl. (That's what I'm like today, just adult-sized!)

Our childhood home in Lee, Massachusetts.

Then, *Bam*! Without warning, they brought Krista home from the hospital. When she got home, I cried. She invaded my space, kicked me, poked me, and drooled all over me. She forced me to share life with her. I made her hold my hand all the time. We got used to it. What other choice did we have?

A twin's life is pretty awesome, though. Our identity would be one from there on out: the Twins. Whenever I spoke or Krista spoke, it was always "we," not "I."

Mom dressed us in the same outfits but in contrasting colors, probably so she could tell us apart (instead of looking closely at my fat face). I imagine dressing us up was fun. We were fair skinned, blonder than blond hair, blue eyes: cute and adorable. Mom would stroll us in the old-fashioned baby carriage down Main Street. We always

The terrible two, 1972. Krista, then me holding her hand. See how fat I am?

attracted attention. (Or maybe Mom was so hot that *she* attracted attention. It's a toss-up.)

Identical twins are considered freaks of nature, mutants, while fraternal twins are considered normal. That's what science says. Did Darwin ever study twins? What's he got to say? Krista and I don't seem to fit into the theory of natural selection—maybe survival of the fittest, since there's two of us. Nature does latch on to mutations that will guarantee survival. And believe me, being Krista's little sister, I was always in survival mode. When divine intervention messes with things, science labels it as unexplained: mutants! Okay, whatever. We're adorable mutants.

Krista and I had our own language; it probably began in the womb, not verbal or anything super intelligent, just feelings. Our communication was mostly through the eyes. We would identify the same, intangible characteristics in people. I knew what she saw and she knew what I saw. Sometimes in group conversations, we drifted off into similar thoughts, or our eyes met with identical thoughts and then we began to laugh. I think it was sort of annoying to people. But we meant no harm or disrespect; it was just a twin thing, an amusement and a unique, unspoken connection. Without minding, we'd often talk over each other, finishing the other's sentence.

So why are you reading a book about two adorable twin girls, you may be wondering? In addition to cute, we were also unnaturally courageous and playfully daring—a sign of things to come. It turns out that the way we were raised, along with our innate mischievous twin spirit, made us world-class competitors, overachievers, and instilled in us the courage to stare down some pretty demanding challenges.

Krista was the initiator of our adventures. I was the cautious and thoughtful (but always willing) co-conspirator. As toddlers, we lived an adventurous and full life. Naptime was when we were most creative. More than once, we snuck out of our room and into Mom and Dad's, out the second floor window, onto the roof, and shimmied down the pole that holds up the entryway overhang to freedom. The escape route was just outside the kitchen window where Mom would be sitting at the kitchen table, drinking a cup of coffee, having a smoke, reading the *Penny Saver*, or talking to her friends on the phone—taking a well-deserved hour break from tending to her overactive identical twin girls. Her break quickly ended when she saw her three-year-old girls escaping from the second floor, fleeing like well-trained, professional firefighters down the back entryway portico's two-inch steel pole!

Our destination and objective wasn't extraordinary: we just wanted to play outside, run in the grass, swing on the cherry tree branches, pick dandelions, ride our tricycles, or throw the driveway rocks around. That's all! Nothing unusual.

Whoop, there goes one girl! Whoop, there goes the other girl.

"Oh my Gawd! What are those twins up to now?" I can just hear her in her thick Boston accent. Poor Mom!

She quickly extinguished her cigarette, ended her phone conversation, sprinted out the back door, and scooped up her escaping convicts.

Hiding in the bedroom cabinets was just another way Krista and I passed the time. When Mom came to wake us from our afternoon nap we were gone—hiding! Never giving ourselves away. Mom was panic-stricken, had Dad and the entire neighborhood looking for us everywhere. Everyone thought we had been kidnapped. Eventually they found us. I don't remember getting in trouble for that. Or for sneaking out of the bedroom, through the hallway, around the corner, and into the bathroom to spread baby powder and squirt toothpaste all over the bathroom floor and walls.

Our antics weren't reserved just for naptime. One frigid, snowy, early morning we locked Mom out of the house in her long flannel nightgown and slippers. She was fetching the spaghetti sauce from the closed-in porch. Mom and Dad often stored leftover food on the porch in the winter. New England winters are wonderfully cold and the outdoors was a natural refrigerator. We wouldn't let Mom back in. More accurately, we didn't know how to let her back in. We were little, didn't know we had locked the door.

Mom ran next door to Peggy's house, to see if she could offer any help. The two of them coached Krista and me to turn the key in the opposite direction we had turned it, unlocking the door. Mom was back.

Making our older sister Sherri disappear wasn't hard either. Without resistance she crawled into the large antique wooden toy chest. Not just any chest. This chest had traveled from Hamburg, Germany, to New York City by boat on May 20, 1937, via the "Hamburg Amerika Linie" with Uncle Paul, Dad's father's brother. Uncle Paul was a native Austrian who appreciated America. The chest's final destination was Lenox, Massachusetts, where Uncle Paul emigrated. Krista and I playfully lowered the cover and closed the latches.

Good thing Mom found Sherri. She could have suffocated.

Today that chest sits in my family room. I had it restored. According to the professionals, it's rare and a piece I should keep forever, hand-made from trees indigenous to western Austria that don't exist anymore.

Just like our playful mischievousness, our athleticism began at early age as well. One day, when we were using our cribs as trampolines, they broke, becoming wedged against the door. Naturally that produced loud, ominous crashing noises that made Mom and Dad leap to their feet and run upstairs. Dad had to take the door off the hinges to get in the bedroom. He and Mom entered the room and found a cyclone had hit. The curtain rods were bent from our attempts to climb out of our cribs, and our clothes were scattered throughout the room. To make things worse, Vaseline and diaper rash paste were rubbed all over everything, and I was trapped in my broken crib. After all, what are baby girls supposed to do when they are locked in a room for hours? Napping was not an option, just an activity we probably didn't understand or appreciate.

Dad loved our behavior; he actually encouraged mischievousness, daring physical attempts, courageous or risky performances, and anything else we did. He had us flipping off the clothesline, skiing in the backyard at the age of two, balancing on the roadside guard rails, walking the ornate, lime-rock walls constructed next to the perfectly built sidewalks often found in the lime belt of Massachusetts, performing acrobatic stunts from indoor and outdoor pool diving boards, hiking to the fire tower at the bird sanctuary, diving off the rocks into the brisk North Atlantic Ocean, climbing trees, doing cartwheels in the house, practicing round-off back handsprings in the yard—I could go on forever.

Mom, however, didn't revel in our daring and curious behavior like Dad did. She ensured that we had a more sane home life, but fun nonetheless. We'd eat ice cream before dinner, and she'd send us out to play in the rain in our bathing suits. We watched *Sesame Street*, ate at McDonald's on our birthday, pizza on Friday nights, got balloons and a parade when we learned to use the toilet, baked cookies, and went to Laurel Lake so we could swim with the minnows.

She was also no-nonsense, though, particularly when I was a little loose with my tongue. Her solution was to wash my mouth out with soap. Pasty, bubbly, chalky yuck filled my mouth. I gagged. When she was finished scrubbing I spitefully rinsed her effort to tame my spirit with a glass of tap water. My mouth was squeaky clean, though—for a little while anyway. Erich, Krista, or Sherri—none of them got their mouths washed out with soap, just me.

She knew how to manage my sassiness too. When I was about ten, I told her I was going to run away from home because things didn't go my way. She said, "Okay Kimmie, can I help you pack your bags?"

I let her help me pack my bag. Suitcase in hand, I confidently left the house eager to face the world. I made it up Laurel Street about two hundred yards before I realized my future looked grim, lonely, and scary. I headed back home. I'm sure Mom was watching out the window the entire time. She did welcome me back with a hug and a kiss. She may have even helped me unpack. I don't remember.

One day when we were teenagers, Mom indulged our curiosities. Her favorite sister, Suey, had taught her to smoke when she was thirteen. Krista and I thought it was cool to smoke. We were inquisitive, asking Mom several times if we could smoke. Of course she always said no. Until one time, she said, "You girls come ovah here. Wanna smoke?"

Reluctantly (because we knew smoking was bad for us), but with the excitement that comes from doing something naughty, we said, "Yeah."

"Come ovah here to the sink, hold the cigarette in your mouth, take a strong, deep breath and make shore it fills yah lungs," Mom said.

Krista and I looked at each other, and our eyes communicated a positive reassurance; simultaneously we smoked the cigarette.

Goodness gracious! We felt like Death was at our doorstep. We could hardly breathe, coughing up smoke and tar, our eyes watering uncontrollably, we dry heaved into the sink, noses running, and angry that Mom had intentionally inflicted such pain upon us.

She was in hysterics, laughing, trying without much effort to soothe our agony.

I would never ever smoke again.

Mom and Dad worked very hard in many different ways, and were sure to include us kids—there was a lot to be done. The garden and the firewood were the two major chores Dad gave to keep us busy all summer and fall. Mom provided us a fair share of work too: dusting, vacuuming, keeping our room clean, and washing the dishes after supper.

The combination of Mom's and Dad's childhoods influenced how they would raise us. Dad grew up on a farm in Austria, and as you can imagine had lots of chores to do each day. I always feel the pride he radiates when he talks about the prized cows he raised, or the crow, Hans, he and his mother taught to fly back and forth from the wild for a piece of bread, or his loyal farm-hand, a black-and-white Appenzeller Sennenhund named Bless, who would herd the cows, sheep, and unruly chickens with the precision, intelligence, and agility Dad admired and respected. Time marched on for Dad, and in 1961 at the age of nineteen he decided to travel to America where his Uncle Paul, Opa's (Dad's father) younger brother, was living. After being drafted by the US Army in 1964 and serving until 1967, he became a US citizen.

L to R: Uncle Edwin, Bless, Aunt Marianne, first generation prized cow, Oma, second generation prized cow, third generation prized cow, Dad, Opa in the background.

Mom, the youngest girl in a family of seven siblings (six girls, one boy), was the offspring of an Irish mother and a Swedish father. She and her brother and sisters were raised near the ocean, north of Boston, in a busy and bustling household where everyone had to pull their own weight.

To Krista and me, our garden appeared huge, twenty-one feet wide by thirty-six feet long. We began learning the farming trade at the age of six. First, throughout the garden Dad spread real cow manure, which he got from Ed the farmer on Golden Hill. After the manure cured for a while (stopped smelling), we got to ride on the front cover of the Gravely tractor while Dad rototilled the garden.

The only thing that kept us on that tractor and not chopped up in the tiller was a firm octopus-like death grip we had on the hood of that Gravely with our tiny hands and feet, plus a lot of will power. Every now and then, Dad took one hand from the controls to ensure we stayed on. Otherwise we'd be goners, mixed up with the dirt and cow manure.

When the weather forecast looked favorable, we planted the garden under Dad's tutelage. We took the top end of the hoe, turned it upside down, and dug it gently into the prepared soil to make rows for the bush beans, carrots, peppers, beets, and cucumbers. We laid the seeds, covered them with the dirt pushed aside from the tiny trench, and watered the rows of what would become fresh vegetables in a few months. The cauliflower, squash, and zucchini had a slightly different planting procedure. They required circular trenches on square dirt plateaus instead of straight rows. The pole beans and tomatoes were planted in individual holes. Once they grew to about six inches, we inserted poles next to the plants for climbing support.

Planting was the easy part. But tending our food source was the hardest and most important task. Summers were hot and humid—good for growing a garden, but tough on the labor force—which consisted of Sherri, Krista, and me. Watering, weeding, and pruning we did several times a week, in between playing with our neighborhood friends.

Mid to late August was harvest time. That was endless work. Picking beans, cleaning and then freezing them—over and over again until at last Mom or Dad decided we had enough beans. You'd think when the freezer was full, we had enough. Nope, not always the case. Once, before Dad gave us the okay to stop picking, Krista and I made the decision to pull every row out of the ground and throw them into the compost pile. Loads of beans were still on the bushes. We pulled those bean bushes with malice and without remorse. I have no regrets.

I felt like I was looking at mountains when the brown grocery bags overstuffed with bush and pole beans that we had picked were dumped onto the kitchen table for cleaning. I couldn't even see Krista's face on the other side of the table. It took *hours*. But we got through the bean harvesting unscathed and the better for it. By the way, fresh, unwashed beans from our garden were really, really tasty, not to mention exceptionally healthy.

Have you ever plucked a tomato right off the vine you planted, pruned, watered, and personally nurtured? Firm but juicy, bright-red tomatoes full of tiny seeds were always wonderfully luscious, and Mom's homemade spaghetti sauce is still *delicioso*. But boy, sometimes Mom was mad as a hornet when she made that spaghetti sauce. It was an all-day event in the scalding hot, humid air. You needed to either stay away or follow Mom's every direction like a well-trained soldier. Submerging my tiny, clean fingers and hands into the warm but cooled blanched tomatoes was gooey and fun. That's how I got to taste the sauce at every stage of the process and be Mom's wingman for the day.

Our cucumbers were prickly and scratched my skin. Mom

would turn those menacing veggies into succulent, crunchy pickles that were stored over the winter in the cold cellar. Squash and zucchini were the easiest to harvest: just pick 'em. A firm, half-inch twist and they snap from their ground-level vine. Carrots were a cinch too. Grab the five-inch fuzzy green leaves and pull. The carrot's mud and dirt pours off and back onto the garden. Bits of loose dirt were still pasted to the orange vegetable, but I'd brush it off with my earth-stained hands and start chomping on the carrot like Bugs Bunny. Beets were also an easy harvest, just a firmer tug. They needed weeding and watering periodically like all other veggies. And I couldn't just bite into a raw beet: they're bulletproof. Preparing succulent beets requires talent. Dad makes a beet salad that rivals any five-star New York City chef.

Since we had a wood stove, we harvested wood, too. It saved money and kept us fit and warm throughout the winter. On Saturdays in the late fall, Krista, Sherri, and I loaded into the front seat of a green dump truck Dad borrowed from someone at work. Dad was a machinist, who learned his trade in Austria and perfected it in Switzerland. His specialty was the lathe. The Berkshires area was well known for paper mills, and pumped out a lot of paper and a lot of pollution. The company Dad worked for manufactured the machines that produced the paper.

We headed out to the woods. Once Dad finished cutting fallen trees with a chainsaw into manageable pieces, we loaded the wood into the truck bed and headed home. The ride was bumpy. We all smelled like wood and chainsaw gas. Dad raised the bed of the truck while we looked on, directing him how to unload the wood safely and in a precise location in the backyard. That self-assigned task made me feel important.

After Dad split ALL the wood by hand, we piled it. ALL of it. Well, okay, almost all of it. Poor Sherri seems to have gotten the brunt of that chore. Not because she was told to pile it all by herself, but because Krista and I took to fighting, which only prolonged the already time-consuming chore and put poor Sherri's life in danger. Krista made me angry or maybe I made her angry—I'm not sure. When we fight we fight: punching, hair pulling, tripping, head locks, shoving, pushing, and anything dirty, even throwing wood. We began chucking wood at each other and paid no attention to who or what got caught in the crossfire. Sherri had to dodge the flying wood, and soon enough got so fed up that she told us to go away. We weren't proud of our behavior. She never told on us, just continued to pile the wood until the job was finished, or Mom came outside and said, "Sherri, where are those twins? Why are they nawt helping you?"

Poor Sherri shrugged her shoulders and continued the manual labor. I'd rather work in peace than be in fear for my life too. That's why she took on the brunt of that chore.

Fighting so violently was a twin thing too. Any feelings, especially negative, were physically expressed directly and immediately. Krista and I would punch each other's lights out. Then within minutes we were friends again, like nothing happened.

Our neighborhood was the type that kids yearn for—it was safe and close to town. Families with two to four kids made up most of the households. Easygoing elderly couples made up the minority. The parents were all friends and kept an eye on each other's kids. Moms would gossip over coffee or on the telephone. Dads went to work. We played kickball and football, rode Ski-Doos in the winter, swam in one of the three neighborhood pools, and rode our bikes everywhere. We liked to ride our bikes up and over Circular Avenue, through the grass, behind houses, down sidewalk stairs, with no hands, through anyone's yard, over curbs (which provided the opportunity to do a wheelie), or down the paved street into the lipped dirt driveway that launched us inches (and felt like feet) into the air and dropped us into the Jaouens' backyard (The Jaouens were one of the few senior couples living in the neighborhood.) Mr. Jaouen would slowly, always with the same gait, stroll from his house through his yard to his garage, on his way to do an errand for Mrs. Jaouen. I'd hit the ground with both wheels speeding past him on my way home. He didn't seem to care; he probably adored the rambunctious kids careening through his yard every day.

My bike was forest green with a banana seat, and U-shaped handlebars outfitted with playing cards clothespinned to the wheel spokes for sound effects. To further accessorize, I had white streamers hanging from the handlebar grips too.

One time I was riding with no hands, flying down Circular Avenue, and didn't make it to Mr. Jaouen's driveway. My bike spun out on the paved street's loose gravel. I don't know what happened next except that I was splattered on the pavement. My bike was twisted in all directions and my knee and elbow were gushing blood. I swiped my blond hair from my face, and held my right knee tight to stop the bleeding, then removed the rocks and pavement embedded in the newly acquired hole adjacent to my kneecap. I brushed the sand off the rest of my limbs, stood up, and walked over to unmangle and pick up my distorted bike. I was alone, holding back tears and whimpering, limping home and pushing my bike through Mr. Jaouen's yard. The scar on my right knee remains prominent (among the others I would acquire over the next ten years).

Winter or summer—the season made no difference to the amount of fun we had. One frigid winter day we divided our neighborhood gang into two teams, probably boys against girls, and built barricades out of the plowed snowbanks. We huddled behind the safety of those frozen walls and assembled our arsenal of weapons—snowballs! Bundled up toasty warm, but freezing nonetheless, we played war.

Bullet after bullet hurled through the air. Seldom was anyone hit. But Michael was a good pitcher and had a wicked fastball. Once, I popped up above the protection of my snowbank, cocked my arm, took aim to launch my weapon when, without warning, I was down, hit by a 90-mph ice ball (Okay that's an exaggeration. It was probably only going 60 mph.). Smack! A direct hit to my right eye. I cried. It stung badly. I was hurt.

When Krista's your sister, these sorts of things don't go unpunished. She jumped over the wall faster than any flying ice ball that day and had a few "words" with Michael. Then she walked back over to me and said, "C'mon, Kim, let's go home and get you fixed up." She wrapped her protective arm around me and we walked home. The game was over—for us, anyway. The other kids probably kept playing.

Michael never messed with me again.

Every weekday before school, around 7:30 a.m., our neighborhood posse played kickball at the bus stop. About thirty minutes later and after a spirited three or four innings the bus showed up. The kid in possession of the ball scooped it up, while the rest of us ran to grab our backpacks and then loaded single file onto the bus. Krista and I often showed up at school a little messy, with one knee sock halfway down, white blouse untucked from the plaid jumper, our neckties twisted, hair uncombed, perhaps a little sweaty, but always obedient and ready to learn. The nuns never commented.

Since Dad was athletic, sports were a big part of our lives, especially skiing, gymnastics, soccer, and swimming. When Dad was a young man, his neighbor in Gaissau, Austria, said to him, "If you have kids who are athletically talented, do everything you can to nurture that gift." As a result Dad taught us every sport he could and entered us in any local competition available for little girls. Mom wasn't a sports enthusiast or a competitive participant, but she could hold her own. She was an adorable tomboy back in the day, and used to play "powda puff football" in her hometown of Beverly, Massachusetts. According to her she was good, real good. I believe her. Krista and I usually won in whatever sport we competed in, placing better than all the boys in our age group and often age categories older than our own.

Our first ski competition was the Snoopy race at Jiminy Peak. I remember that one well. I was nervous; I had no idea which way to go around the poles. Of course Dad instructed us how to do it, but I didn't pay attention. Luckily, the race organizers traced blue dye from the start to the finish along the entire race route just for kids like me. That was a relief. However, I forgot to go fast. That's why Krista won; she got a trophy, and I got nothing. The picture of her holding her very first trophy and me standing next to her like a cute loser hangs on my refrigerator. It's clear who the winner is: Krista, the scrawny, chicken-like one, trophy in hand. I'm the one who fills the ski suit well, almost busting out of my outfit, and empty-handed.

1974

A few years later Mom and Dad packed up the yellow VW bus one early Saturday morning and drove us to Pico, Vermont, for our first out-of-state little kids' ski race. Dad knew we were pretty good so he thought he'd expose us to the opportunity. Plus everyone in the ski racing world knew that Vermont was where ski racers could thrive and excel.

It was a big hill. Everything was intimidating. But Dad had a way of convincing us that we were just as good as anyone there. When you train hard and dedicate yourself to something, you lay a foundation that's solid and always backs you up. He never used those words, but later in life, I got it. The challenge was fun, and the trophy may have been superficial, but it was symbolic.

I was in the starting gate on top of the largest ski mountain I had ever been on in my entire young life. My attitude was focused: *Go as fast as you can, Kim.* I rocketed out of the start gate like the McDonald's Hamburglar after stealing a hamburger, speeding through the course. I crouched to a tuck position when necessary, and opened up just in time to carve a turn around the gates. My loose, oversized, borrowed Ski-Doo helmet bobbed up and down throughout my entire race run.

The next thing I knew, halfway through the course I was hurling through the air like a snowball, then tumbling over the snow-packed ski slope like a rag doll, before finally sliding to a stop. With both my ski-pole straps around my armpits, I got up, ran lopsided with one ski secured to my ski boot to fetch the other ski, which was lying along the route of the racecourse, and jammed my ski boot into the snow-packed binding. Twisting each of my pole straps so that I could grab hold of the grips, I reentered the race. I reached the finish line in one piece—sort of.

Mom was in the finish corral, hysterical. "Kimmie, Kimmie, honey, what happened to you? Are you okay?" she asked while hugging me tight. "Oh my Gawd, Elma!" Dad's name is Elmar.

It's an Austrian name. "I'm gonna kill him," she said, like any caring, panicky mother, upset because my nose was bleeding, and blood soaked my frostbitten face. Snow was packed in between my eyes and behind my crooked and cracked goggle lens. Only one ski pole was with me. The other one must have escaped in my fleeting effort to reach the finish line as rapidly as possible. My well-fitting ski suit was coated with loose snow and frozen blood.

I had no idea of my outward appearance. All I knew was that I got to the finish—a loser, again.

Dad came skiing beautifully down the mountain next to the racecourse, proud of his little girls. He always dropped us off at the start, and gave us some inspiring encouragement—a word or two, nothing confusing or long-winded, then skied to the optimal but inconspicuous viewing area.

"Kimmie, what happened?" he asked compassionately, but stunned. "You skied great."

Each tended to me, Mom with the touchy-feely, nurturing reassurance, Dad with his stoic words but compassionate facial expression. To Dad, being stained with blood, weeping crocodile tears, and seemingly a disaster was no big deal, just part of being a little girl. To Mom, it only confirmed her fear of the crazy behavior Dad promoted. Krista, calm as a cucumber in the distance, shoulders propped over her ski poles, impatiently waited beyond the finish area, probably wondering what all the commotion was about. Finally, she skated over to let me know I was fine and say, "C'mon let's go." We went to the base lodge to eat our homemade, packed lunch.

I sulked all the way home in our yellow VW bus.

Krista probably won the race. Neither of us remembers.

———

Dad had us playing and perfecting every European sport possible. Mom didn't care much about sports, as you know. As a matter of fact, what we did often frightened her. But she got involved when we wanted to play farm team baseball (farm team was a level below Little League) or take ballet lessons.

"Dad, Krista and I want to play baseball?" I asked, knowing in his mind that American sports were inferior to European sports.

"I don't dink dat's a good idea. You girls don't need to be playing baseball," he convinced us in his thick Austrian accent.

"Elma, if those girls wanna play baseball, they are gonna play baseball." Guess Mom was in charge this time.

Not skipping a beat she said, "Get in the cah, girls. We're going down town to sign you up."

Dad, balding already, in his short workout shorts, T-shirt, and European clogs, walked toward the garden, shaking his head. He had no more say. We were signed up and on a team.

I played shortstop and catcher. Krista was the pitcher and played first base. Boys and Missy Croze filled the rest of the positions.

Missy was up to bat. She got a piece of the first pitch, but fouled it. Second pitch was a fastball. I don't think she even saw it.

"Sssstttrike!" the umpire said with devilish pleasure.

Disgusted, Missy slammed the tip of her bat on home plate, then swung it over her right shoulder. She propped her left hand on her hip, stood firmly facing the equally confident, dorky boy pitcher, and yelled in her squeaky, commanding, pre-teenage voice—complete with stink-eye aimed directly at the entire opposing team—"Hey. Don't pitch the ball that fast. Slow it down." I'm pretty sure that boy didn't slow it down.

That was coed farm team in Lee, Massachusetts!

Krista and I weren't limited only to action sports; we wanted to take ballet lessons. But Mom didn't have the money, and Dad wasn't going to fork out the cash for *ballet*! Aunt Jane (Uncle Paul's American wife) came to the rescue. The class, like every little girls' ballet class around the world, included adorable little girls dressed in pink leotards, pink ribbons around bouncing ponytails, pink ballet slippers, and annoying moms around the perimeter of the studio.

The class began with a gentle warm-up and stretching, followed by the many disciplined movements and positions of dance. The most fun of every session was when the entire class, led by the teacher, pranced around the studio pretending to be one long butterfly. We even performed in a recital on stage! I loved ballet.

Dad went to every baseball game and even the ballet recital. Of course Mom did too.

Mom got a call from the principal at Central Mental, that's what everyone called the public elementary and middle school in Lee. The alternative was St. Mary's Catholic School. Kids who went to St. Mary's were called St. Mary's fairies. Sherri went to Central Mental. Krista and I were St. Mary's fairies, and Erich started out as a St. Mary's fairy but completed seventh and eighth grade at Central Mental. I don't know why, but I think it's because the nuns couldn't handle him. Erich brought fireworks to school and lit them off at recess. He and his best friend, Andy, got caught climbing onto the school roof. Erich's bike was impounded by the nuns for an entire week because he failed to heed the multiple warnings not to do wheelies through the school parking lot. And in second grade he put tacks on a girl's chair. She sat on them. But I think what really got Sister Barbara upset was the nature-appreciation project he turned in, a picture torn out of a *National Geographic* magazine of two animals in an

African wildlife reserve openly engaging in the act of reproduction. Mom said she and Dad let Erich transfer to Central Mental so he could participate in the woodworking class and play the drums in the school's marching band. Neither class was offered at St. Mary's. Erich said that the transfer was a mutual agreement between him and Sister Barbara, the school principal. Okay, whatever! Can you imagine a sixth grader negotiating with a Catholic nun? I don't think so!

Anyway, the principal at Central Mental called to tell Mom that Sherri fell off the jungle gym during recess and needed to go to the hospital. She'd broken her ankle. And for rehab, the doctors suggested she swim. So Dad took her to the YMCA. She joined the swim team and ended up being one of the Y's best swimmers. While Sherri practiced with the swim team, Dad took Krista and me upstairs to learn gymnastics. Dad was a very good gymnast who'd learned everything he knew from a club in Switzerland before he moved stateside.

The Y swim team coach needed the youngest age category kids for his upcoming meet. He asked Dad if his twins wanted to participate.

Dad said, "Sure."

Next thing I knew I was doing lap after lap in the Y pool; breaststroke, backstroke, freestyle, and practically drowning as I valiantly tried the butterfly. We learned flip turns, proper technique, starts, and the plethora of swim competition disciplines. I got my first blue ribbon competing in a Y swim meet. Finally! I wasn't the habitual loser anymore.

Sports were becoming important to us—not just because we won trophies and ribbons, but because the experiences were fun and meaningful. Improving and learning made Krista and me feel good, and it was why we looked forward to our after-school and weekend practices and competitions.

Dad was keen to our talent and as a result nurtured it. He knew our motivation and disposition were unique and that we were different.

CHAPTER TWO
Losing Us

One day when we were about twelve, Dad sat us down and said, "You girls are very good at sports. But if you want to be really good, you need to pick one sport and concentrate on being the best. Take a few days, talk about it. Let me know, and then we'll work really hard at it."

The place that helped expose us to a variety of sports was Eastover, located in Lenox, Massachusetts. It was founded in 1947 by an Italian immigrant named George Bisacca, and was a 457-acre year-round recreational vacation resort—sort of like the place in the movie *Dirty Dancing*, but with way more sporting facilities and not at all elite or reserved for the upper class. Eastover had six tennis courts, indoor and outdoor swimming pools (both with diving boards), a sauna, horseback riding, running trails, a basketball court, a baseball field, outdoor volleyball courts, an ice-skating rink, a bobsled run, four ski trails, a rope tow and a chairlift, hay rides, archery, bonfires & marshmallow roasting, pedal boats, mini golf, three holes of regular golf, skeet shooting, safari rides in the buffalo refuge, shuffleboard, horseshoes, and kiddie land, a day camp for kids.

Happy hour was poolside each afternoon, and Tally Ho was a party spot, renovated from an old horse stables, where the night came alive. Live music was performed on a rotating bandstand. Dancing, pizza, hot dogs, and soda started about nine p.m., and went until the wee hours of the morning. It was a BYOB resort.

Dad was a lifeguard at Eastover when he'd met Mom, who was in her early twenties and vacationing with girlfriends at the resort. Mom and Dad hooked up and got pregnant with Krista and me. We were an accident (it took me until I was about forty years old before I got smart and did the math to figure the whole thing out), so they got married. I'm sure they were in love; it's just the sequence of things was out of order. Mom already had six-year-old Sherri from a previous marriage.

Mom & Dad's wedding day, October 26, 1969.

Dad had a sleek black Porsche, but had to sell it in order to finance his new, lifelong investment: a wife, a young daughter, and a baby. The fact that we were twins neither one of them knew about until eight months into Mom's pregnancy. Mom went for an X-ray (there were no ultrasounds back then) and the doctor said, "Oh, wow, there's a lot of hands and legs in there!"

Mom was beside herself, distraught, scared to death, not knowing what was wrong with her baby. "Oh my Gawd, is that baby okay?"

"Judy, I think you are going to have twins," the doc said.

Fear took on a new meaning at that point. She would never be the same again. Dad wouldn't either.

Serious cuteness. Schmidinger Family 1972. Do you know which one is me? I'm on the left.

While raising their family, both our parents had second jobs at Eastover. Mom was a stay-at-home mom during the week and a waitress on weekends. Dad was a full-time machinist and a life-guard at night and on weekends. Since Mr. Bisacca liked Mom and Dad, Eastover was our playground, literally, when mom and dad had to work. Krista and I even got to ski during times when kids weren't allowed. Heck, at Eastover Krista and I got to do whatever we wanted all the time.

On the slopes at Eastover, 1973. I'm on the left, ensuring Dad holds my hand. Krista, already a daredevil and independent. George Bisacca and his daughter, Susan, in the background.

Often Dad made us tidy up the pool area before we ventured off to whichever activity suited our mood that day or night. After dumping the ashtrays, picking up empty soda and beer cans, plastic mixed-drink cups, and used towels from the grounds and lawn chairs, we were free to roam, play, and discover to our hearts' content.

On summer days, lunch was served poolside for guests. Krista and I somehow finagled fried shrimp and milkshakes. At night, Dad delivered us turkey dinners. I shouldn't be saying that because "the help" wasn't supposed to be eating food intended for guests. But that's the way it was!

Soda was on the honor system. When a guest checked out, they told the front desk how much soda they'd drunk and were charged accordingly. Anyone could take a soft drink from the many unattended soda bars located throughout the estate. We never abused it, because we knew soda wasn't good for us. But it was fun to stand at the bar, scoop a cup of ice, pop open a can, pour a Pepsi or an orange soda into the clear plastic cup, and drink it.

Mr. Bisacca was a tall man, somewhat stiff in the upper body, gentle yet domineering. He reminded me sometimes of an Indian chief; at other times he appeared to be more like a well-respected general. He was a Civil War buff and kept a spooky museum on the estate called the Heritage Room. Beyond the museum was a spacious area for group and family gatherings, card playing, movies, or warming up between ski runs or after ice-skating. Sometimes when Mom and Dad worked late, we watched TV in the scary Heritage Room. And since I was curious, sometimes instead of watching TV I spent the evening discovering and studying all of the staged sets in what was known as one of our nation's largest privately held Civil War collections. At night it was ghostly. I thought everything might come alive.

There was a life-size display of Abraham and Mary Todd Lincoln at Ford's Theatre when poor Abe was shot by the famous actor and Confederate sympathizer John Wilkes Booth. There were battlefield sets complete with stretchers, blood, prairie and emergency medical wagons, bayonets, campfires, horse-drawn carriages and so much more. Black and white mannequins were intricately dressed in Civil War attire. Some were dead, with blood coating their bodies. Others were alive—standing, kneeling, or lying in strategic fighting positions. Groups of soldiers huddled together in war-like planning circles. Weapons, cannons, and all sorts of other period paraphernalia filled the Heritage Room. There were even jails and Indian sets complete with teepees, squaws, bucks, and babies wrapped in native costumes. It was all there, a wonderful history lesson on display for guests or staff to savor and learn.

Eastover also hosted all kinds of special events: Civil War reenactments, cannon shooting, themed meals, costume contests, archery and shuffleboard tournaments, pool parties, the Special Olympics, after-prom and birthday parties, reunions, field trips, company outings, breakfasts with Santa, and community swim lessons.

Grand floats of times gone by were hand-built and entered in the Lenox, Massachusetts, Fourth of July parade. Beautifully dressed horses mounted by Mr. Bisacca accompanied by his two daughters marched in those parades.

Thousands of people from all over New England have happy memories from Eastover etched in their soul. I can't imagine growing up without it. But more earth shattering is that Mom and Dad would never have met and we wouldn't be here if it wasn't for George Bisacca's Eastover.

As time went on, Eastover became our training grounds. Krista and I spent many hours playing tennis, running, hiking the grounds, skiing, and swimming laps there. While we ended up putting most of our energy into skiing, what I was drawn to was ice skating. Though there was no proper ice-skating facility, no club, and no coach, there was an untended outdoor rink at Eastover that was permanently ripped out before I knew it. But when Eastover's rink (or the frozen ice after a winter rain storm outside our house) was available, I would gracefully and athletically perform with heart and passion, teaching myself moves I had seen on TV. I'm sure I wasn't very good at ice-skating. But I thought I was.

Regardless, every sport was fun. Winning, losing and the challenging training sessions had their own unique rewards, even when we were middle-school age. Like the time when I got a flat tire during one of our long bike rides. Krista was ahead, as usual. I could see her constantly pulling away. Dad often stuck with me, riding behind or in front so I could draft, or he even rode next to me so he could give me a push every now and then.

He'd always sprint ahead, ensuring Krista got the support she needed in order to maximize her potential. Then he would slow up enough for me to catch him. I didn't need a flat tire to set me even further back.

I sat on the side of the road and cried; tears rolled down my cheeks. Dad cuddled next to me, strung one arm around me and said, "Kimmie, we'll get your tire fixed. Don't worry about that. You can beat Krista. All you have to do is ride a little harder and a little smarter."

I listened.

The next long bike ride I rode a little harder and a lot smarter. As we climbed the tough hill from Stockbridge Bowl (a lake), to the Lenox monument in the center of town, I drafted Krista tight. Just as we crested the top of the hill I dug down deep, pedaled extra hard and passed her like she was standing still. Dad said that was a turning point for me.

In the end it came down to skiing. That's the sport Krista and I would pursue. I don't recall having any extra passion for skiing, but I think Krista dominated our decision, which was fine with me. I was a happy follower most of the time.

Serious ski training began on the slopes of Eastover. Mr. Bisacca let Dad set up gates for us when the ski lifts were shut down at night or after school. Since the lifts were closed, we had to hike back up the hill after the many training runs. It wasn't so bad. The slope was all ours! No hoodlums to interfere with our training course.

We were also members of the local Bousquet Ski Club, where Dad was a ski instructor and continues to be a club coach—forty years later. Every weekend and one night a week we trained with the club, learning and repeating proper ski techniques and racing skills. After interclub, we aged into the United States Ski Association (USSA) program, racing regionally and always placing in the top three.

Night training at Bousquet was often cold, and of course, always dark in the winter. We skied under the lights, which felt different from the day. There was also a thrill in getting to stay up late. Krista and I plus Heidi, our teammate, pretended to be well-known American ski racers like Tamara McKinney, Heidi Pruess, Cindy Nelson, or Christine Cooper before each training run. During chairlift rides, Heidi would make me laugh, tell funny stories, and imitate Animal from *The Muppet Show*. She always had a lot of energy.

When we were twelve, loaded with Hubba Bubba chewing gum, bags of powdered Lipton iced tea, and a few bags of Toll House chocolate morsels, Mom and Dad put us on an airplane headed for Zurich. We were going to spend our entire summer vacation in Dad's hometown of Gaissau, so that we could better understand Dad's culture and practice our German. Gaissau is a typical tiny Austrian village in Vorarlberg, perfectly constructed and meticulously kept. It borders the Bodensee, Europe's largest fresh water lake. The Bodensee is 833 feet deep and 149 miles around. Germany, Switzerland, and Austria surround the Bodensee.

Traveling without our parents to Europe was becoming a family tradition: Sherri went, then Krista and I, and eventually Erich, all when we were young teenagers. The airline personnel paid close attention to our well-being, and escorted us on and off the airplane. Aunt Marianne, Dad's older sister, picked us up in Zurich.

We'd been to Austria twice before with our family to visit our grandparents, and were well-versed in the German language, since that's what Dad most often spoke to us. Our grandmother,

Oma, was Swiss. She was a tough nut who grew up through two world wars, but was as generous as generous could be. She was mischievous, though. Whenever we visited her in Austria, or she and Opa visited us in the United States, she was always slipping us Swiss francs and Swiss chocolate right before bedtime. In Austria, when the family was brewing their schnapps with the village distillery that traveled from house to house on wheels, she would give us a schnapps glass, tell us to go outside, fill the shot glass with the pure, warm, freshly distilled pear and apple schnapps, straight from the still. When no one was looking, she motioned from the second floor kitchen window to drink it right down. "Only one shot," she would say with a sweet scold to her favorite eight-year-old American grandchildren.

On a Swissair flight from Boston to Zurich, 1978. Erich, Dad, Me, Krista.

Krista and I slowly tipped our glasses to our mouths, then swiftly gulped every drop. It warmed and burned our throats on the way down and tickled once it settled into our stomachs. We wiped our lips with the sleeves of our shirts like it was no big deal, hopped on our scooters, and away we went. Drunk! Just kidding.

(To this day I can drink schnapps with the best of 'em, but any other alcoholic beverage, not a chance. I'm a lightweight and a cheap drunk, and Krista, too, although she likes to occasionally puff on a cigarillo. I guess after all these years, she forgot about the perilous smoking experience Mom put us through.)

Believe it or not, during one of those family trips I saw an angel in Oma and Opa's living room. Really!

While everyone was gathered around Aunt Marianne and Uncle Gottfried's kitchen table, eating, drinking and carrying on, I meandered over to Oma and Opa's house (over time Oma and Opa's farmhouse had been converted into a duplex). Curious, I opened the door to the living room to admire the little Christmas tree. That's when I saw it. It was pure white, a flicker almost. Shaped like an angel. It radiated gentleness, purity, softness, and peace. It didn't see me. I moved closer to discover, and as I moved boldly but innocently, she caught me looking at her. The angel was startled and gone in a flash. *Puff*, just like that, and I never saw it again. I won't ever forget that experience and still believe that what I saw was a real, God-created angel. Today that angel watches over me all the time.

Aunt Marianne and Uncle Gottfried, a Zollner (an Austrian border guard—who knows everyone and everything) had four children. Andrea was our age, Heidi a few years younger, and the two boys were little tykes. During our later summer trips to Europe we hung out with Andrea every day. The three of us rode scooters or bikes, raided the local farmers' strawberry patches, pedaled across the Austrian/Swiss border over the Rhine River to the public pool in Switzerland, bought chocolate at the village grocery store, picked up fresh, warm, milk in a metal canteen every evening from the farmer down the street, threw stones at the windows of the boys' houses in the neighborhood, listened to Casey Kasem's Top 40 on the radio, and zipped across the Austrian/Swiss border on our bicycles whenever we felt like it, waving at the uniformed, armed border guards—seldom having to stop for inspection because of Uncle Gottfried. But every once in a while a Swiss border guard motioned his index finger at us to come over, then stopped us and asked what we had in our bags. Duh, Swiss chocolate of course! Andrea practiced her English, Heidi didn't, and Krista and I practiced our German.

To keep up with our physical training, almost every day Krista and I went on twenty-five-kilometer bike rides around sometimes flat or mountainous, often hilly terrain, or took twenty-minute runs on the dirt roads through the flat, open farmland that eventually joined the Bodensee. Spending time with family and friends engraved in our being that we fit right in. European culture and the people were second nature to us, familiar. We were just like them. These trips to Europe would prove invaluable.

One winter during a USSA Tri-State region ski race at Bousquet, Dave Ojala from the prestigious ski academy Stratton Mountain School, in Vermont, along with Albert Arnaud (pronounced *Ahl-BARE Ar-NOH*—he's ALLL French) from Dynastar skis, came to scout three young, hot ski racers from the unlikely state of Massachusetts: Heidi, Krista, and me.

I had no idea they were there, but they were impressed with our performances. Not long after their visit, Krista and I were offered a five-year scholarship to one of the country's best winter sports academies, compliments of Stratton Mountain School and several ski equipment sponsors. Located in South Londonderry, Vermont, Stratton Mountain School is a college preparatory academic and athletic institution for young people aspiring to be exceptional Alpine or Nordic skiers, freeskiers or snowboarders.

But Mom wouldn't allow us to board at the school, as she would have no part in her girls living without direct supervision, and insisted on some sort of home life. Without that, we would not have been attending Stratton Mountain School, period. Mom had put her foot down, again. So together my parents expressed their concerns to the headmaster and coaches, who suggested that we board down the road from campus with the Beardwood family, whose daughter Holly was attending Stratton Mountain School. The Beardwoods were glad to have us. Mom and Dad moved us into their house, where Krista and I shared a cozy four-bunk room, complete with our own bathroom, with Holly, who was a year older than us.

Once we were settled, Mom and Dad reluctantly but courageously left us. At the young and impressionable age of fourteen in the fall of 1984, we became winter-term students at Stratton Mountain School. I was scared, insecure, homesick already, and cried for hours. Krista didn't cry. She probably wanted to, but I was doing enough for the both of us. Dad said Mom cried the entire two-hour drive home too. Mom said she cried for two weeks, not two hours like Dad thought. It must have been heart-wrenching—losing us at the age of fourteen to a talent Dad had encouraged and nurtured.

We spent November through March away from home training under a spirited and determined, heavily accented Austrian coach named Fritz Vallant. Fritz had my back—for as long as he could anyway! Krista and I welcomed the daily schedule, appreciated the teachers, and blossomed within the environment at Stratton Mountain School. Most of the kids were like us. They were athletic, goal-oriented, and focused. It was where we needed to be in order to grow as athletes and as people.

Each day at Stratton, with the exception of one day a week, we began the morning at six thirty with an early morning run or some type of exercise. Seven a.m. was breakfast. Eight a.m. until eleven a.m. was ski training. Noon was lunch. One p.m. until five p.m. were academics. Six p.m. was dinner. Seven p.m. until nine p.m. was study hall. We competed on weekends.

One week of every month, every student—whether we were full term, winter term, a campus resident or day student—was assigned kitchen duty. That meant a team of about five students reliably took on the task of cleaning up after the roughly one hundred students and faculty had finished each of their three meals every day for an entire week. I learned how to run a commercial dishwasher, spent time scrubbing pots and pans, mopped the tile floors, placed the clean dishes and silverware back on the shelves, wrapped and stored leftover food, wiped the tables, and vacuumed the dining area. Sometimes water fights broke out, and the job took a little longer than usual as a result. It was teenage-like to complain about kitchen duty, and sometimes it interfered with my typical daily schedule, but in hindsight, I remember it fondly, and it taught me the value of working together. Kids who attended Stratton Mountain School came from diverse social and economic backgrounds with varying levels of athletic and intellectual talents. During kitchen duty, athletic ability, brains, who your parents were, and money were irrelevant. Completing the job quickly, cooperatively, and precisely was the goal.

Academic classes were small, with six or seven students per class. My teachers were exceptionally smart but easygoing—it was Vermont, after all. Vermonters tend to wear flannel plaid shirts, Carhartt pants, earmuffs or a hat, carry warm coffee mugs around all day, and have beards. The relationship with the faculty was always personal and family-like, but discipline and focus were never left out of the equation. Not even for a sweet, innocent, Catholic girl like me. I managed to get kicked out of class twice by two different teachers.

Len, the very tall, gangly, bearded math and science genius, didn't appreciate my drawing of a ski jumper launching off one of his graph handouts. I thought it was funny, and so did Flash, the Nordic skier sitting next to me. While Len, coffee cup in hand resting on his protruding belly, lectured us on something to do with the Introduction to Physical Science, I elbowed Flash to take a look at my ski jumper. He looked over, chuckled, and marked up my graph with his very own jumper out-jumping my jumper. We both laughed under our breath. Len heard us. He didn't like it.

"Kim, you can leave," Len scolded *me*—not Flash, just me.

Oh my God! I thought. *He's always liked me. He doesn't mean it. He's joking.*

Len was not joking.

"Really Len, you're kicking me out of class?" I asked in my sweetest, humblest voice, while my eyes and cheeks begged for forgiveness and leniency.

He pointed to the door. He was NOT joking!

I left, a scolded, embarrassed puppy.

That was a horrible experience. I'd never gotten in trouble before, except from my parents, naturally. I'd always been a shy, respectful girl. As soon as I saw Len, I apologized. He gave me a one-arm hug (because he had a coffee cup in the other hand), almost breaking my shoulders and snapping my ribs. Big guys seldom know their own strength.

But I didn't learn my lesson.

Before I knew it, the exceptionally fit, bowlegged, often disheveled German teacher named Jani (pronounced *YAH-nee*), a gentle Scandinavian, was telling me to leave his class too. All I was doing was secretly being engrossed in the tales of my *Soap Opera Digest,* which lay what I had thought was imperceptibly inside my open German textbook, while pretending to read the day's lesson. I already knew how to speak, read, and write German; Dad taught me. What was the big deal?

To Jani it was a big deal: a disrespectful big deal. Again, I begged for leniency in my sweetest, humblest voice. It didn't work this time either. I left his class, a scolded, embarrassed puppy for the second time, as he confiscated my *Soap Opera Digest. Oh Geez, is he going to give me my magazine back? I haven't finished reading it,* I thought. Instead I apologized and never got in trouble at Stratton Mountain School again, except for one last time, sort of.

Everyone in our class was either exceptionally smart—like going to Middlebury, Harvard, Dartmouth, St. Lawrence, Williams College smart—or a world-class athlete. Some were even both. We were a model group of young people: brown-nosers, Goody-Two-shoes, or whatever you want to call us. Therefore the faculty and athletic staff weren't expecting to have to bail us out of jail for the possession of marijuana, our senior prank.

We had devised a plan to be caught for something we didn't do. A few of our classmates were local, so they knew the town police and asked if they would be accomplices to our senior prank. They agreed. Six or seven of us, including Krista and me, were picked up off campus by the Londonderry police in the Sun Bowl, where we were "caught smoking pot." We were stuffed into the police cruiser and driven back to school. The cruiser stopped during lunch, right in front of the large dining room windows. The uniformed cop got out, opened the back door, and escorted us into the building, through the media room adjacent to the lunchroom, and directly into the headmaster's office. It was hard to keep a straight face. But we did, including the police officer.

The students and faculty eating lunch looked on in dismay.

With our heads down, we took seats in chairs and on the floor of the headmaster's office. The door was shut behind the last senior class delinquent. The police officer, the headmaster, the assistant headmaster, several faculty members, and a coach or two joined in. Silence filled the room for a few very long moments. Many of us snuck our eyeballs up at each other hoping to catch a glance of reassurance or a smirk of accomplishment. We listened as the headmaster sat at his desk, arms folded neatly in front of him while he scolded and lectured us with incredible disappointment in a soft and devastated voice.

He said something like, "Many of you are in the midst of outstanding athletic careers, or on your way to Ivy League schools, and all of you have promising lives ahead. A police record makes some of these things impossible. What were you all thinking?"

No one responded. Silence dragged on. Then, a few students were called upon to answer. But no one spoke, only shrugged their shoulders.

Holy cow, we have really got these guys fooled! They believed the spectacle, and we were pulling it off. The headmaster excused all of us, not knowing what to do next. I felt sort of bad. They were genuinely hurt by our supposed behavior. After all, Stratton Mountain School is a small, tight-knit, caring community. A place dedicated to nurturing bright, talented young people. Of course our teachers and mentors felt a deep pain, and a sense of failure.

We had never considered their feelings during the planning stages of this prank. After all, we were teenagers, who rarely consider the consequences or the feelings of adults.

I don't know who, but that day someone told the headmaster the truth, that we never smoked pot. It was all a prank. I'm sure he and the entire faculty and staff were angry, maybe even embarrassed, but in the end relieved.

That was the class of 1988's senior prank, and the last time I did any practical jokes or pranks at Stratton.

Larry, the English literature teacher, didn't think I was all that bad. He taught the dreaded beginnings of English literature. That meant we had to read the epic poem "Beowulf," Chaucer's *Canterbury Tales*, Shakespeare's *Romeo and Juliet*, and Bram Stoker's *Dracula*. I liked his class. Not necessarily the material, but the way Larry presented and taught those impossible forms of literature. He was intriguing, wacky, animated, and funny. I laughed inside a lot. He spoke to us as if he was each character in the books. The words came alive, gaining my attention and engaging my interest.

Later, Larry became Stratton Mountain School's headmaster and awarded me the headmaster's award for winter-term students. Imagine that: me? I'm an athlete, and not supposed to win academic awards.

Athletics at Stratton Mountain School weren't any different from the academics. The relationship with my coaches was also personal and family-like. Discipline, dedication and focus were paramount. When we were no longer the responsibility of the faculty, the coaching staff took over. Fritz ensured productive and tough training sessions, on and off the hill. He even gave me a hard time once because I had ditched swim training. I told him I had an obligation to finish a project for French class. He thought I didn't know how to swim, and that's why I wasn't going to training. Clearly he didn't know about my Y swim team experience, the blue ribbon, or my training at Eastover.

Most importantly, Fritz believed in me and my skiing

abilities. He told me there are three kinds of people, "Those who watch things happen, those who let things happen, and those who make things happen." His tone and demeanor assured me that I was the latter. Following a poor performance on the hill, he would tell me, "After a rainy day comes a sunny day."

I was always inspired to perform with that kind of feedback.

A certain amount of flexibility was okay at Stratton. Schoolwork could be rearranged when a competition interfered. Every once in a while, it was okay to work out with Sverre and the Nordis (Nordic, or cross-country, team). Working out with high-level Nordic skiers was no easy task, especially when I wiped out while trying to maneuver a slight and gentle descent on cross-country skis, but it made for a refreshing change from my usual alpine routine. Fritz didn't like my detours, but always went along. I got to make decisions and be active in the direction of my future. That was important.

Winter term at Stratton was only for six months. So from April until October, Krista and I returned home and resumed our education at Lee High School. The principal and faculty at Lee High embraced our unique path, and had prepared six months of the year's curriculum that the teachers at Stratton Mountain School taught to us in classes with additional winter-term students.

At home, soccer was our other sport. Ms. Maish was the caring and dedicated coach of the Lee High Wildcats, the women's varsity soccer team. My senior year, we became the Berkshire County Champions. Our soccer team from the working-class town of Lee beat out the Lenox Millionaires (named after the town's erstwhile summer residents, like Edith Wharton, Nathaniel Hawthorne, Herman Melville, and the granddaughter of Commodore Cornelius Vanderbilt, Emily Thorn Vanderbilt Sloane), the Taconic Braves, the Monument Mountain Spartans, and six other high schools in our district. Krista was the league high scorer.

Dad knew that becoming a successful ski racer wasn't only about skiing. He understood that overall physical fitness was critical in preventing injuries or illness, optimizing training and competition performance, maintaining the stamina for the competition season, recovering from the long, strenuous season, and being one step ahead of the competition. Together, we devised a five-day-a-week program that included running, soccer, tennis, agility, coordination, balance sessions, swimming, hiking, road biking, canoeing, and track workouts. Often Dad worked out with us. Other times it was just Krista and me.

Sometimes Krista and I didn't feel like exercising. In that case, we pretended to go on our run through the woods behind the house and up Circular Avenue, only to detour to our friend Michael's house. (Remember Michael? He's the one who hit me with an ice ball when I was little.) We hung out with Michael and his brother Colin, sometimes played Wiffle ball in his yard for thirty minutes, and then pinched our cheeks to make them red, sprayed water on our faces and in our hair to make it look like sweat, and then jogged back home.

When we weren't off ski training for two weeks at a time on a glacier in Europe, a volcano in Oregon, or dry-land training out West, we spent the summer months in Lee working at Eastover as waitresses. We saved our earned money and used some to buy incidentals during our trips.

"Dad, how are we supposed to get to work?" we asked.

"You have two nice refurbished bikes in the garage." (Since Dad's a machinist, he likes to rebuild things.) "You can ride them to work, do your job, swim some laps in the pool after work, then ride your bikes home. It's the perfect way to incorporate your dry-land (off-snow) training into your daily schedule," he explained.

We rode our bikes five miles each way to work each day.

Most of the time, working at the restaurant was fun. The chefs were all really nice guys, most of the time. But once John, the executive chef, made me cry when I used the wrong coffee spout while preparing my guests' dessert order. I suppose when there's pressure to feed two seatings of prime rib or turkey dinner to five hundred people, tensions rise and foul language flies.

Suddenly out of nowhere, John sprinted toward the coffee urn, pushed me out of the way, and whipped the coffee urn handle back to its closed position, while I was routinely filling a coffee pot for the guests at my table.

He then said, "You idiot, the coffee is still brewing! Don't you know that?"

I stood dumbfounded.

Well . . . no, I didn't know that because there was no Styrofoam cup over the handle, is all I was thinking. We were taught that when the coffee is still brewing there's ALWAYS a Styrofoam cup covering the handle, indicating to the wait staff that the coffee isn't ready to serve or there's nothing in the gargantuan, scalding hot urn that's supposed to feed the five hundred guests.

John was in a rage. I was startled and had never been yelled at like that before.

I walked with my head down through the kitchen, which was buzzing like a beehive with activity, to hide my red face and the tears that were about to burst from my eyes. I found solitude in the dessert kitchen, where I busied myself gathering my tables' dessert orders. My tears eventually rolled over my cheeks and dripped into one of the guests' strawberry shortcakes. I threw the contaminated dessert into the rubbish as though it were John, pulled myself together, and delivered the desserts to my guests with a smile and said, "I'm sorry, but you'll have to wait for your coffee. I just got yelled at by the chef. He won't let me get any coffee right now. It shouldn't be long, though."

They understood, or they were drunk and didn't care much about their coffee. Having fun and camaraderie was why people visited Eastover. Rarely, if ever, did guests give the wait staff a hard time.

Every October, the Eastover kitchen and wait staff had a Halloween costume contest. Mom always dressed up, often taking the top prize of fifty dollars. Krista and I participated one year. Krista was a clown and I was a bag of jellybeans. That was Mom's idea. A large clear plastic bag surrounded me from my neck to my knees. Mom, Krista and I blew up colored miniature balloons, dropped them into the bag, and painted my face.

Well, I showed up to compete and wouldn't you know it: the dirty-minded, filthy-mouthed male chefs and waiters were convinced I was a bag of condoms.

The judges awarded me third place—fifteen bucks. Yay me! As far as I was concerned, I was still an innocent bag of jellybeans. It didn't matter what the distorted competitors thought. Perhaps their slanted inference made me even cuter in the eyes of the judges!

Stay the course.

CHAPTER THREE
The Team

As young teenagers, Krista and I had established ourselves as the top junior alpine ski racers in the United States Ski Association's (USSA) Tri-State (Massachusetts, Connecticut, and Rhode Island) region. But being the best from Tri-State meant that we might be in the middle of the pack against the Vermont, Maine, and New Hampshire kids. That was the thinking in the world of junior ski racing in New England. Dad knew better. Our first year competing in the Junior Olympics (eastern regional championships), Krista and I placed in the top three, and Krista even won one of the events. We then performed consistently in the top five of Eastern Cup competitions during our first year attending Stratton Mountain School. As a result, we had secured national rankings that qualified us to be named to the United States Alpine Ski Team's National Training Group at the age of fifteen. Of course these results and accomplishments were exciting. They made us feel good, eager to keep training, and reaffirmed our impressionable self-confidence, but the seeds to reach these kinds of accomplishments were laid by the lifestyle we'd grown up with. It began the day Mom bundled us up in snowsuits and Dad strapped our tiny feet onto skis and ran us up and down the snow bank he'd built in the backyard when we were two years old. Earning a spot on the US Ski Team was a natural progression. Sort of like beating the boys.

Being members of the US Ski Team was a roller coaster of

emotions, relationships, and schedules. It was an experience filled with achievements, failures, fun, and disappointments. Vertically, horizontally, and diagonally we zipped around the world by car, van, train, subway, and airplane, training and competing; we didn't even know that we lived and learned in a protected and sheltered microcosm of world cultures. Everything except incidentals and personal items was paid for by the US Ski Team, which is a branch of the United States Ski Association, the privately funded national governing body of US Olympic skiing and snowboarding. Airline tickets were mailed to our home address for our convenience (back in the day before digital ticketing on the Internet!). November was like Christmas, when our team uniforms were handed out. We were branded with sponsor logos from head to toe, whether we liked it or not. Itineraries, accommodations, transportation, travel companions, and even what we ate were planned by someone else.

It was a harsh environment—a "Me, Me" mentality. Results typically moved individuals forward. However, progressing up the ladder wasn't always based upon performance. Some athletes got preferential treatment. Discretionary spots were awarded. Rules, criteria, and promises didn't always hold true with the team. Winners of timed runs didn't always compete in the promised competitions. Winning a title didn't always guarantee the spot you earned. Character wasn't important. Some athletes proved mischievous, disrespectful, self-centered, and dishonest. A few walked to the beat of their own drum, oblivious to their surroundings but well aware of who and what to step on. There was nothing I could do about any of that, except continue to perform.

Of course, many teammates, coaches, and support staff were kind. Some were funny. Many girls created lifelong friendships, and some found their soul mates. Regardless, Krista and I were lucky to have each other.

Coaches were fired, promoted, or proven unreliable before I could even count on them. This was another reason it was good to have Krista around.

Our first World Cup competition, Park City, UT, 1987. I placed 23rd in the giant slalom. Guess again: who's who? Krista's on the left.

And yet I wouldn't change growing up this way for anything. Most of our friends in Lee went to the prom, participated in school clubs, hung out downtown or at the roller rink on Friday nights, prepared for college, and all of the other wonderful things American kids do growing up. What we did was just different.

Our first US Ski Team on-snow training camp was at Killington, Vermont, where the best fifteen- and sixteen-year-olds in the country were brought together for a week of training. I was nervous and intimidated by the unknown. We sized each other up: some girls were shy, others were bold, mean, competitive-looking, fun, or just plain unreadable. A few were friendly. Some could really ski, but most weren't anything to worry about, because they didn't appear to be exceptional. We were placed in groups and assigned to coaches who free-skied with us and ran us through an array of technical drills. The training camp was all about having the chance to meet and interact with other gifted athletes.

As the winter season progressed, hundreds of talented girls were winnowed to a small core group who eventually traveled and competed consistently together for several years. Tanis, Gibson, Krista, Monique, Julie, Sally, and I made up the Europa Cup Team or National Training Group in the mid-eighties. Each of us had discipline specialties. At first Krista and I excelled in all five categories: slalom, giant slalom, super G, downhill, and the combined. Slalom and giant slalom are considered technical events that focus on shorter, quicker turns at top speeds of 25 mph in slalom, and up to 50 mph in giant slalom. Super G and downhill are considered speed events that focus on long, high-speed turns with courses containing jumps, flats, dips, and compressions. Speed event skiers reach speeds of 70 to 80 mph. Technical events have more gates that are spaced closer together, whereas speed events have fewer gates spaced farther apart.

As time went on, our performances and the team's needs steered us to become specialized. A few psychologically and physically damaging crashes in the downhill discipline left me scared to death and scarred for life. One of them occurred when I was about seventeen years old. I timidly exited the starting gate of a Nor-Am downhill competition at Steamboat, Colorado. Nor-Am, or the North American Cup, is a competition tour organized by the International Ski Federation (FIS) in the United States and Canada. The Nor-Am Series is a level below the FIS World Cup and equivalent to the Europa Cup in Europe.

The initial terrain was flat, but my mind was racing. I knew I had to get in a tuck and let my skis effortlessly glide and swim—that means the skis wiggle horizontally, supply back and forth over the surface of the snow. The thought of catching an inside edge, which would slam me face-first into the snow, or catching an outside edge, which would twist me in an awkward and tangling position, was terrifying. I was intentionally gaining momentum and speed, knowing full well that steep terrain was ahead. Then three jumps, one directly after the other. *Oh God, how far apart are they?* I couldn't remember. They were big, though; I knew that. If my entry onto the first jump wasn't executed properly, then the second jump would launch me like a rocket and land me square on the top of the third jump—which was exactly what happened. After miscalculating the precise location of the first jump, I landed just prior to the takeoff area of the second jump—off balance, and with all my weight on the tails of my skis. My speed, which was fast, quickly launched me off the second jump. I flew straight up, ski tips curling over my head, my arms wind-milling in desperation, thinking, *This is going to hurt.*

Gravity eventually brought me back to earth. The tails of my 215-centimeter skis hit the snow first, then my cushy butt found land. My head, thankfully adorned by a helmet, slammed back against the snow, and I bounced a few times as I skidded and tumbled down the racecourse. One ski exploded upon impact; the second released from my ski boot. One of my shins absorbed the brunt of the impact as I came down cockeyed. My ski poles were somewhere many yards above me.

My body was intact, nothing broken or torn. But I was in shock. Dizzy. A team trainer assessed my condition and determined that I had sustained bruising on my shin. Well, duh! By the time I got back to my hotel room, my shin was swollen and brightly black-and-blue, and I had a hard time walking. My elbow annoyingly hurt and wouldn't bend or straighten smoothly. Regardless, with mechanical movement I checked it out in the mirror. Severe bruising encircled the back side of that joint as well.

No one considered that I might have had a concussion.

Eventually I found the courage to refuse to compete in that crazy, death-defying event, much to the chagrin of my coaches. They thought that with a little more training and competing I could be good. Well, with a little more training and competing like that, Evel Knievel would have had a female counterpart to contend with.

I did, however, love slalom, giant slalom, and super G, while Krista thrived on the rush, the speed, and the jumps of downhill. She was equally competent in all other disciplines, but to fill the US Ski Team's need for a promising downhill team, she dedicated her time to the speed events and sacrificed the practice time she needed to maintain the skills for the technical events.

A blond, friendly guy from out west was our very first Ski Team coach. Early on, I thought he had my back and I could count on him. Eventually he was promoted to athletic director, managing every sport within the jurisdiction of the United States Ski Association. Then the seven of us were no longer his priority or sole responsibility, and I began to realize that we were just athletes who were supposed to make him or whichever athletic director came next and the entire organization look good. A new set of coaches was hired. Replacing the staff would become the norm. We rolled with it.

And we rolled with minor and major injuries too.

We were training on the Rettenbach Glacier in Solden, Austria, in October at another fourteen-day training camp, and for weeks I'd been nursing an injured ankle from playing varsity soccer at Lee High School. It was nothing so severe that it should keep me off the snow. Or should it have?

On-snow training started at eight thirty a.m. I took three training runs in the super G course. That went well. The next two runs would be timed, determining unequivocally where we stood. The clock isn't subjective. It's an accurate ranking. I liked that. On the first timed run I skied well, but missed a gate near the bottom, so the run didn't count. No big deal—I was determined to put in a good time. I headed back to the start for the second timed run. My ankle, however, was sore.

Out of the starting gate I went with a few swift, strong pushes and several long skates. A moderate flat dictated a tuck in order to be aerodynamic and reach maximum speed. I initiated my turns tenderly because the snow was soft, and I didn't want to sink into the snow, which would slow me down. I smoothly transitioned my weight and foot pressure from the tips of my skis through the arch of my foot to the skis' tail. The buildup of energy released and rocketed me forward down the fall line. Every turn thrust me faster and faster to the next gate. I was accruing momentum. The air wrapped around me. I was a bullet.

Up ahead the terrain shifted to a long, steep pitch. Memorizing the course was helpful to me, as well as looking ahead, anticipating and feeling my movement. I lifted my chest slightly up and forward, rolled my hips over the toe pieces of my bindings in anticipation of the terrain change. My weight was distributed between my toes and the balls of my feet, arms tucked closely in front of me, but still in a supple and aerodynamic position to firmly ensure my balance.

Swish—over the bank I sailed, catching a little air. My stomach was light just before I delicately touched down and continued gliding securely on the surface of the lightly packed snow. It was steep, and the turns were getting tighter, and the gates were coming quicker. I loosely held a tuck. My movement around the gates was a strong, fast, angulated carve. Everything was moving rapidly.

In an instant, I was caught off balance; I'm not sure how. Before I knew it, my weight twisted backwards. My hips dropped behind my heels, my arms opened up, leaving me vulnerable to disaster. I was losing balance. Gravity yanked me sideways, instead of effortlessly complimenting my intended and controlled downward direction. I used the strength of every muscle, ligament, and bone in my teenage body to avert a catastrophe and regain proper position. But that was not happening. My ankle was weak, setting off a domino effect throughout the skeletal structure and soft tissue of my body. *Snap* went my knee! My strength failed me. Physics pulled me down the fall line. My body complied in a wringing motion that rendered me helpless. I tumbled head over heels a bunch of times.

Splat! Face down, motionless, I was lying covered in glacier snow, one ski on, one ski off. I clearly failed to reach the finish line for a second time. I inventoried the situation. Slowly I ran energy from my core to my limbs. *I'm okay.* I got up. *Wait a minute, my left knee is not working properly.* I slowly set pressure on it a second time. It still wasn't holding me up.

With assistance from my coach, I got off the hill and back to the hotel. The team doctor thought that I'd added injury to my already sprained ankle and torn my medial collateral ligament in my knee. That usually means surgery and definitely no skiing for some time.

I was bummed and shed a few tears. But I was sixteen and full of energy, determination, and confidence, and naive enough to think that any obstacle could easily be jumped over, crawled under, or simply walked around. Whether the situation was easy or hard, I faced each experience with confident optimism. I most often called home when I had performed well, sometimes when I needed a shoulder to cry on, or in this case when I was injured. Mom and Dad were heartbroken and considered traveling to California with me. But I assured them there was no need.

I was put on crutches, and the injured knee was secured

in a metal-lined, oversized brace that was strapped from my ankle to my groin. Not very fashionable, and my movement was minimal. I could take the brace off to ice or bend to prevent muscle cramps. It was two days before the team could get me a flight to Lake Tahoe, California, to see Dr. Steadman, the US Ski Team's chief orthopedic surgeon. I was driven to Zurich and dropped off at a very nice hotel, where I spent the night. I had clear, empty plastic bags to ice my knee, bars of Swiss chocolate, my journal, and a stuffed animal neatly packed in my carry-on.

The next morning, I took the hotel shuttle to the airport. I checked in at the SwissAir counter, then hobbled through the Zurich airport with a backpack hanging from my shoulders to the departure gate. I flew cramped in economy class to Boston, my first scheduled stop before reaching Lake Tahoe. Seven hours later, I transferred to another airplane that took me to Denver, where I switched airplanes again. I was headed to Reno, Nevada, almost my final destination.

The team had arranged for my teammate Eva's mom to pick me up, since she and her family lived in Reno, about an hour from the Barton Memorial Hospital in Lake Tahoe. Eva was still back on the glacier in Solden, training with the rest of the team. Her mom was a short, friendly but stern lady with a Polish accent. The slot machines ringing and blinking caught my attention as I came out of the airplane. *In an airport?* I thought. She took me home to her house and put me to bed. Talk about exhaustion. I had left Switzerland around ten a.m. Swiss time, shuffled halfway around the world by myself, arriving twenty-one hours after my first flight's departure.

Eva had already won a silver medal in the World Championships at the age of nineteen and took flying lessons. She had a waterbed in her room. I'd never slept in a waterbed before. It gurgled and flowed all night. I woke up several times, scared

that the brace I had to wear 24/7 (yes, even to bed) would puncture the mattress and spew water all over Eva's room. The next
morning, Eva's mom fed me breakfast, and then put me in a car
that took me directly to the Barton Hospital in Lake Tahoe.

I met Dr. Steadman. He was tall with a big build, soft-spoken,
and gentle. I could tell he was a thinker. He examined my knee,
pondered things, and then seemed to come to a quick decision
in his head. Then with a model knee, he thoroughly explained
the surgical procedure I needed. He ensured that I understood
and felt comfortable with what was going to happen.

Little did he know that I was good to go—just wanted to get
through the surgery, start rehab, and get back on the snow as
soon as possible.

I was prepped for surgery by a skinny, pleasant young nurse
named Crystal. Still exhausted because I was on European time,
I was strolled into surgery at seven p.m. to repair my left knee's
partially torn medial collateral ligament. They knocked me out,
because I didn't want to comprehend the intentional slicing of my
skin and carving around in my body. That's gross. Plus a few hours
in oblivion would be good for me. I could catch up on my sleep.

I wasn't afraid at all until I woke up dazed and groggy in the
cold, sterile recovery room with a single window that looked at
a concrete wall. There was not a soul around. I was hooked up
to an IV, some type of monitor, and had no feeling in either of
my legs. The experience was creepy; it almost felt like I was the
victim in a horror movie. A large institutional clock hung on the
wall. It said nine p.m. I went back to sleep.

The next morning, I was dragged from my bed with a stiff,
sore knee and guided by my own manual power to the rehab
center. I felt woozy and weak all over.

The rehab staff, who were well trained and dedicated to
getting world-class athletes back to competition as soon as

possible, patiently but adamantly walked me through my rehab exercises, performing them alongside me. They included:

1/3 knee bends (both legs)
1/3 knee bends (single leg—good leg)
linebackers
straight leg raises
quad sets
1/3 knee bends with stretch cord
4-way ankle-straighteners
15-minute stomach routine
5-minute easy warm-down—stretching

That afternoon, the rehab guys put me through the same training session again. I was more alert that time. They told me I'd be out of competition for eight weeks. That's two months! The competition season started in mid-November, and I wouldn't be back on the snow until Christmas! That was upsetting.

Just stay positive, Kim. It's only a speed bump, I thought.

After the second workout session, Dr. Steadman took me home to stay with him and his wife for a couple of days. The powers that be assured my mom and dad that I was in good hands and would be well taken care of. I was.

I woke up the next morning at eight a.m. Pacific Time, lost. I had no idea where I was. Didn't know what town, state, or country I was in. The room was unfamiliar. It felt like it was the afternoon. Confused, I got out of bed and limped around tentatively. I wasn't sure if my legs were strong enough or if my head was cognizant enough to keep me upright.

"Oh," I finally realized. "I'm at Dr. Steadman's house. Okay."

No one was home. I found the kitchen and looked around for some breakfast. I sat at the kitchen table eating minimally, because I wasn't sure what I was allowed to help myself to—if anything. After a few bites, I began to feel light-headed and exhausted. Jet lag, surgery, painkillers, pain, anesthesia—it all had caught up with me. I sat at the kitchen table like a statue for a while. When I slowly began moving, I felt like a Mack truck had hit me. Everything creaked as if I was the Tin Man in *The Wizard of Oz* needing oil after decades of stagnation.

Still dizzy and almost checked out of reality, I did my rehab routine on my own in the living room of the Steadmans' house. The guys at SPORT (the rehab clinic) had told me to, so I did. But the real rehab started at one thirty, when I was taken back to the rehab center by one of the trainers. I warmed up on a stationary bike with my good leg (my injured leg didn't have a range of motion yet. Plus the four orthoscopic incisions needed time to heal and close up. Everything inside my knee probably required delicate treatment too.) My battered leg, still numb and the size of a cantaloupe, was propped up on a chair, loaded down with a bag of ice. It was wrapped tight and snug with gauze, an Ace bandage, and a protective, unattractive brace that allowed a controlled, shallow range of motion.

After the warm-up, I pedaled one-legged again, this time for ten minutes with amplified intensity and resistance. The intervals intensified to sprinting with thirty seconds of recovery in between, and finally a warm-down. Next I moved to overall body conditioning with a rowing machine and weights. Then the dreaded stretch cord. Mustering up every ounce of mental fortitude, I painfully gritted my way through the battery of stretch cord exercises, which left no muscle or ligament unturned, flexing and strengthening every conceivable inch of my body. This was no time to show my fragile state, even though it was consuming me inside.

The next day I woke up fully aware of where I was and what

lay ahead. Back to SPORT I went, where I did the same grueling workout as the day before, plus my abs received their very own fifteen minutes of exercise.

At sixteen years old, I knew how to work hard. But with a knee injury, I now knew how to work harder. Determination and commitment would surely need to be driven by self-discipline. I left Dr. Steadman's house and my new friends at SPORT on October 25. I was headed home. My connecting flight from Denver to Boston was canceled. The airlines put me up in a hotel and got me on a flight the next afternoon. Sherri picked me up, and we drove home to Lee.

Every day at six a.m. before I went to school and Dad went to work, he helped me with my rehab exercises. Like clockwork, I limped down the stairs in my pajamas, my hair full of snarls and eyes full of sleep gunk, to put in the time and effort to heal and strengthen my knee. Dad never missed a workout and often had to drag my sleepy attitude awake.

After school, I finished the rehab and conditioning that didn't require Dad's assistance. Occasionally too much home-work cut into my after-school workout, so I had to complete the regimen sometime before bed. But I was dedicated. I wanted to be 100 percent when I got back on the slopes.

The month of November came and went with lots of sweat, tears, and progress. There were days when everything went right. And then there were days when I wanted to throw my knee out the window and get a new one. But there was not a day when I didn't focus on getting back on snow.

My teammates, including Krista, were on a busy competi-tion schedule. Nevertheless, Krista and I remained close, sending letters back and forth. A phone call here and there. I missed her, she missed me, but it was a given that I'd be back. We always had a connection, intuitively relied on each other, and performed our best when knowing the other was still in the game, even if an injury benched one of us temporarily. Her performance was my performance, and mine was hers. She was competing well while I was sidelined, but that gave me peace of mind and kept me hungry to return. It's a twin thing.

Eight weeks after my knee and ankle injuries, I flew back to Reno for a checkup. Dr. Steadman gave me the go-ahead to begin free skiing. The very next day, one of the trainers took me to the nearby Heavenly Valley ski area. Mentally I was anxious and apprehensive. At first I skied slowly, methodically, and safely. With each additional run, I delighted in greater momentum toward familiarity, confidence, and comfort. I was on my way, and it felt good.

Every day I looked forward to skiing. Competition season for me finally began stateside in late January, and then we were off to Europe. I started each race back in the pack anywhere from fortieth to eightieth posi- tion, and even dead last a few times, but most often I finished in the top ten, and sometimes in the top five. I was performing to and sometimes beyond expec- tation. That was inspiring and reassuring.

St. Sebastian, Austria – that's me.

CHAPTER FOUR
On The Right Path

A year after we made the US Alpine Ski Team, equipment sponsors and a headgear sponsor provided Krista and me with an annual retainer and a victory schedule (bonus money is awarded for winning or placing in high-profile events). Dad, acting as our manager and with our input, did all the negotiating. For teenagers we made pretty good money, but Dad encouraged us to save as much as possible. Saving our money seemed logical, because life on the road was paid for, and when we weren't traveling, we lived at home or at school.

Every November, the team trained in Beaver Creek, Colorado, for three weeks, in final preparation for the race season. Beaver Creek made snow on their main trail, Centennial, just for us.

Boulder, Colorado, was the perfect place to get away from the intensity of training and truly relax for a few days. Most of us managed to get into some sort of trouble, or at least have lots of fun. On Friday afternoon our coach gave everyone a cash stipend. Off he went, not to be seen until late Sunday, when he rounded us all up and herded his young and talented girls back to the slopes of Beaver Creek.

The University of Colorado at Boulder's football team, better known as CU, was really good at that time. After playing quarters at one of the houses in our buzzed, drunken state, we headed to the football game. From there some of us sobered up, some didn't. Who knows how we acquired tickets. The stadium was packed. Regardless, we were on the sidelines, right on the field, not stuffed in back rows far from the action. I was getting chummy with some short college guy who happened to be a friend of Monique, my teammate. Neither Krista nor I recall his name. Gibson and Krista remember looking up and seeing me hanging all over him. I had a plastic cup of something in one hand, while the other was draped over this guy's shoulder.

Krista thought, "Okay, hmm. Kim looks to be in an odd place for her, but okay, whatever."

You'd think someone would have rescued me from myself! Clearly a few drinks were affecting my better judgment.

The game ended. CU won. We stormed the field. The masses, including our group, took down the goalposts. We zigzagged home, my loyal companion in tow. Eventually we ditched him. Thank God.

While we were contemplating dinner, my newly acquired friend (let's call him Henry—I like that name) called on the telephone, asking to take me to a frat party. I was sober by then. So the answer was definitely NO.

But someone threw out that Krista should go out with Henry and pretend to be me. Gibson, Sally, Monique, and a few other girls agreed.

Krista said, "Hmm, well, I don't know . . ."

Monique said, "He drives a Porsche and he's from Aspen."

Another girl chimed in saying, "I'll give you my stipend money if you do it."

"Yeah, I'll give you my stipend too!"

Before Krista or I knew it, everyone was throwing their money into the pot. I was just relieved, glad to find a solution that didn't involve *me* going out with this guy.

Krista decided that this could be fun, mischievous, and heck, she could make some cash. "Sure, why not!" she said, and looked forward to the adventure.

Henry picked "me" (really Krista) up in a Porsche. They headed to the frat party. Krista saw Anouk, a teammate of ours, at the party. She had no idea that Krista was supposed to be Kim. Anouk tried to get Krista's attention by yelling over the loud, obnoxious music and noisy party chatter.

"Hey Krista," Anouk yelled.

Krista froze and quietly, as quiet as one can be in an obnoxious, loud, crazy, cramped frat house said, "No, no, be quiet. Not so loud. I'm Kim tonight."

Anouk must have been loopy or unable to hear, because she continued on her merry way. Disaster was averted. Krista was safe, cover wasn't blown. Whew—thank goodness.

It was late and Krista was getting bored. She told Henry that she'd like to go, and doesn't remember if she even talked to him the entire evening. Besides the money . . . driving Henry's red convertible Porsche was the other reason she had agreed to go out with him. Krista's not shy. She asked if she could drive home, and he obliged. But not without politely trying to make the moves on her. He sat in the passenger seat like a drooling puppy dog, while she revved the engine, skidded around turns, climbed to the highest speeds possible—everything she could get away with. She dropped herself off, said good-bye, and in the house she went. *Finis!*

We never saw Henry again.

"Tomorrow we'll be having timed runs. The top four results out of six will determine which of you will fill the two vacant spots in the upcoming World Cups," our coach told us.

This became routine. It defined quickly and harshly what it's truly like to be a member of the US Ski *Team*. We were a team, and wanted to be full-fledged teammates. We even liked each other, for the most part. But once we stepped on the hill, the cold hard fact was that we were competing against each other, not just against skiers from other countries or the clock. It was me against them. This was everyone's attitude. We were a group of girls traveling, living, eating—essentially growing up together with a single goal in mind: to win individually at the highest level of world competition. Friendships were secondary, but necessary nonetheless. And like I said, fun was often thrown into the equation too.

Adaptation and resilience became useful characteristics. Sometimes after the spring meetings, world ranking no longer kept you on the team. As the team got better or worse collectively, the criteria to be named to the A, B, or C Team often changed from the previous season. Some girls became victims to these inequities and inconsistencies, and some didn't. Some even benefitted. In one way or another we were all affected, and dealt with it the best way we could. After all, this was world-class competition.

Twelve-hour car rides across Europe or epically long airplane flights from one continent to another, combined with the physical demands of training and competing, were draining, exhausting, and sometimes left me feeling like one big bruise. From limb to limb I ached. Periodically, every part of me had something wrong, whether it was sore and swollen hands from hitting gates with little protection during slalom training, shin splints, a sprained ankle, a concussion from tumbling down icy slopes, muscle fatigue from dry-land training, welts on the back of my thighs from rapid gates slapping back, a broken nose after improperly blocking a slalom gate, and on and on and on. But that was typical for many of us, not just me. You think of young athletes as being impervious to injuries, but the opposite is true. We were constantly nursing the damage that our sport was causing our bodies.

Those words are difficult to pen and tough to accept, but true nonetheless. I didn't consider or realize the impact it was having; it was just part of life. We always sought out the best equipment and protection. Technology and materials continue to create safer environments for sports, but athletes are always reaching higher, demanding more and pushing the envelope. The risks are inevitable and ever present.

Not only did our experiences affect us physically, but psychologically as well. Our three-day trip to Termes de Chillán, Chile, for two weeks of on-snow summer training wasn't solely a nightmare. It was an education in reality. In July, it's winter in South America. Krista and I left my parents' house at ten thirty a.m. and flew from Albany, New York, to Miami, Florida, where the team converged. We spent the night at a Quality Inn, which felt and looked like a 1970s bowler's polyester heaven. But the bed was comfortable. I flicked on the TV to occupy the latter part of the evening. Every fifteen minutes there'd be a live update reporting the newest crime: homicides, murders, drug deals, rapes, beatings—all kinds of brutality. We didn't have that kind of stuff in Lee, not even on the news. It was a gloomy way to spend the evening.

The next morning went smoothly. We boarded the airplane at eleven thirty a.m. in Miami and flew to Panama City, Panama, which seemed just about as safe and drug-free as Miami. That flight took three hours. We then caught another three-hour flight to Santiago, Chile, which included a short layover in Lima, Peru.

Spending the night in one of Santiago's luxury hotels was just what we needed to recuperate from the long trip behind us, and the even longer trip that lay ahead. It almost felt immoral to revel in the luxuries of a fancy hotel in what was then considered a third-world country. But I did, sleeping in a cozy, comfy bed until ten the next morning. I even watched CNN. I always felt more at ease in a foreign country when I could grasp onto anything American: a TV station, an American song on the radio, or even pizza.

There's a level of comfort in America that I never found anywhere else. Just stepping off an airplane, going through customs to have US agents yelling nicely at me to get in the proper line, being called honey or sweet pea by a stranger, is heartwarming and makes me smile inside and light up a little on the outside. Our country's sophisticated organization disguised behind an uninhibited and laissez-faire attitude and sometimes Wild-West demeanor, plus our genuine, unwavering compassion are truly American qualities and what separate us from every other world culture I've experienced.

Midday, we drove into the city center to catch a one-thirty-p.m. train to Termes de Chillán, the ski area. A train in Chile? I remained optimistic. But it was nothing like the high-tech, super engineered, safe trains in Europe. *It couldn't be any worse than the American train system*, I thought.

The Chilean train swayed like a boat. It was old and didn't exceed 45 mph. Six hours of travel by train was supposed to get us to the bus that would transport us another hour and a half to the ski area. Shortly after leaving the station, and feet away from our decrepit, slow-moving train, was my first sight of true poverty. In either direction were neighborhoods of cardboard houses. Roofs were made of tarps, and floors were made from firmly packed dirt. "Windows" were cut out of the cardboard box walls, but there was no glass or screen—just open air. Some windows were draped with heavy woolen blankets. Muddy-colored, stained clothes hung out to dry on lines intertwined throughout the villages. Everyone was dark-skinned and clothed in ragged layers. Their faces were strong, leathery, wrinkled, and proud. Their eyes yearned for a way out. Still, no one begged or interfered with the train.

The day warmed significantly, especially on the plains, but the nights got cold, which explained the dominant smell of burning coal and wood. I photographed every detail in my mind. The sights and the emotions remain vividly within me.

About an hour into the uncomfortable but bearable ride, the train stopped. Food trays were set out, like on an airplane, and we were served lunch. Forty-five minutes passed, and lunch was finished. We were sweltering on the sun-baked, red clay plains of Chile with no air conditioning. The sun beat through the windows of the already hot and crowded train. Just ahead, it turns out, an oncoming train had derailed, knocking out the electricity to the track we were supposed to be traveling over. Two hours passed. Finally someone figured out that the only solution to keep the people on the train from dropping like flies from heat stroke was to send our train back to Santiago.

Everyone was sweating. It was about ninety degrees Fahrenheit, sticky and yucky. Thank God I had shorts and a tank top packed in my carry-on. I changed clothes, but it didn't help much. Finally, we arrived back in Santiago, and waited a half an hour for the train to switch tracks. I decided to amuse myself by laying pennies on the tracks as the trains ran them over. It was neat, and added a brief entertainment for us all.

We filed back on the train, only to look forward to a seven-hour ride. Since we switched tracks, we had to take an alternate route, circumnavigating the derailed train's track in order to connect with the line to Termes de Chillán. Honestly, I don't know how we all remained sane. I suppose we were used to it. Traveling to gorgeous, remote snow-covered areas around the globe was part of the job. (The next month, we would experience a long and obstacle-filled journey from Lom, Norway, to Las Lenas, Argentina.)

At eleven p.m., we arrived safely in the town of Termes de Chillán. We were thankful to get off the train, but stunned to be greeted by messy, begging children at that late hour of the night. They were lively, full of energy and mischief. I got the feeling they had played this role a million times before, and would continue to perform their act a million more. We hadn't eaten in six hours, which made us a tad slap-happy and somewhat impatient, but almost all of us scrounged up our leftover pesos to buy some food at the stand where the kids were waiting with piercing eyes, dirty faces, and a look of desperation, hoping we'd give them some food or leftover change. Their persistence got the best of me and a few of my teammates. We gave them what we had. As we drove away on our bus, the kids ran after us for as long as they could. Each one flipped us off, taunting and yelling until the dust and distance separated us.

The bus was nice, and had a bathroom, reclining seats, and music. We drove farther and farther into what seemed like nowhere. But time passed rather quickly, and we arrived at one thirty a.m. at the ski area, three days after our departure from Miami! Books, a college lecture, a TV documentary, or even first-person stories couldn't educate me the way the Ski Team did during this journey.

The mountain was big and skiing was good when we got the chance. But for the first eight days, heavy rain and wind interfered with training. Each day we fit in some type of training, though, whether it was short course gate exercises, free ski drills, start-and-finish practice, or making adjustments to new equipment. Finally, the last four days of the trip the weather cooperated, maximizing the on-snow sessions. We trained on full-length courses that gave me the opportunity to spend time honing my own technique and getting more acquainted with feel and touch—essentially finesse. Finesse—it's intuitive. When I ski, not only do I automatically apply my life-long on-snow experiences, but I also use my senses, feeling the spatial awareness and understanding the surrounding variables, like the texture and firmness of the snow, the air temperature, the altitude, the weather, and tuning in to my personal disposition rather than using only pure physical force and attitude to perform. The combination of speed and finesse is deadly to the competition.

We left Chile after two weeks. While on a tiny commuter flight from Miami to Orlando, I found myself in a daze, staring out onto the Florida coastline. I was thinking about breathing unpolluted air; smelling the mist and changing leaves on a breezy, cool fall day; walking the streets unafraid after dark; hiking to the top of a mountain and seeing for miles over the vast and dense land below; swimming in a clean, placid lake in the middle of nowhere (but naturally, somewhere in New England); and going to bed at night looking forward to tomorrow. I think I was homesick.

But before going all the way home, Krista and I spent a few days at Disney World. My first priority before hitting the rides, though, was to get clean and find a laundromat. My clothes hadn't been washed in two weeks and I'd been traveling for two days. I smelled, and my teeth hadn't been brushed since I'd left the Andes Mountains. The entire trip from start to finish couldn't have been more diverse. Summer, then winter. Safe, then dangerous. Comfortable then uncomfortable. Rich then poor. Above the equator then below the equator. Reality of all kinds! So different and yet so close.

The adventure, the safety of our protected microcosm, the attention, different cultures, the worldly travel and, in many ways, the friends from foreign countries and throughout the United States, also made this lifestyle special and attractive. Not to mention, it was all I knew. Success though, was the driving force that kept me engaged, motivated, and focused.

The 1987 International Junior World Championships were held in Salen, Sweden, and Hemsedal, Norway. I placed a surprising third in the slalom and fourth in the combined. For a sixteen-year-old, the experience was huge. My composure was mature and relaxed, but sprinkled with nervousness. I had no words for my first international third-place finish, only precious feelings, a world championship bronze medal, a nice crystal bowl, and proof that I was a girl.

Yes, I had to endure the scrutiny of gender verification because the Chinese, the East Germans, and a few other sneakers decided to cheat in the Olympics a few decades back—really! Our team doctor had to complete a form authenticating that I was a girl. Who would have thought that a teenager from a small town in western Massachusetts equipped with female parts and a figure to go with it would be subject to gender verification? In my mind there was no question about any competitor's gender. Naturally some girls were bigger, more muscular, and less feminine than others. But that didn't mean I couldn't beat them or that they were cheating. Yet clearly dishonesty was a part of world level competition even at this age.

In 1988 we graduated from Stratton Mountain School, and a five-year scholarship to the University of Colorado at Boulder (CU) awaited Krista and me, as long as we agreed to ski for their successful NCAA Division I alpine team. That's one of the reasons I felt no need whatsoever to exert much effort while taking my SAT during a day off from November training in Beaver Creek. Our coach loaded Gibson, Krista, and me into a van and headed for a high school in Denver, Colorado, where the team, in cooperation with Stratton Mountain School, had arranged for us to take the SAT. Since ski training was in full force and the competition season was days away, I was in no state of mind to be thinking about academics. About an hour into the thought-provoking yet boring test, I lost interest. I tried to focus for another half hour or so, but the sun pouring in the windows and the snowcapped mountains in the distance carried my mind permanently out of the classroom. I ignored the rest of the test questions, then randomly filled in the empty circles of the SAT bubble sheet. I just didn't care, and my subsequent score reflected it. But I knew our high school grades were good, our reputation was solid, and our athletic achievements had earned us the scholarship that CU had already promised.

Krista and I ended up turning down CU's five-year scholarship, though, because going to college then would have limited our ability to train and compete full-time on the world stage. Focusing solely on ski racing was our top priority. I knew that one day ski racing would come to a screeching halt, and then I would have plenty of time and energy exclusively for academics.

Throughout our skiing career, but more often now that Krista and I were B team members, our competitions were frequently in Europe. Mom or Dad used to drop us off at Boston's Logan Airport several hours early for international check-in. On the hill, off the hill, no matter where we were or what we were doing, the Ski Team's motto is "hurry up and wait." Krista and I took advantage of the spare time and often ventured by subway or water taxi to downtown Boston prior to many evening flights to Europe.

I preferred the water taxi to the subway. The North Atlantic Ocean water smells like nowhere else on earth. The water taxi drops passengers off at Rowe's Wharf, directly in front of the opulent Boston Harbor Hotel. I loved the stroll along the neatly kept concrete waterfront, which meandered under the hotel's magnificent archway, and daydreamed about someday being able to stay there, just once.

We went to Faneuil Hall Marketplace for some chowder and to pick up a load of super-rich, high-calorie chocolate brownies before our flight to Zurich or Munich. The brownies had absolutely no nutritional value, just the comfort of nostalgia, a tangible reminder of America in anticipation of spending weeks in Europe. Staying in hotels in the United States and in foreign countries made it hard to follow a strict or healthy diet. I ate what I was served, most of the time. Chocolate and ice cream were staples and could be found anywhere, in every country.

Ski racing in Austria, Switzerland, France, Germany, and Italy is like football in America. Fans are dedicated, obsessive, loyal, and fanatical. Thousands, many dressed in traditional alpine costumes, line the race routes and finish areas with cow bells, posters, banners, musical instruments, and national pride. Stations of beer, bratwurst, Jager Tee (spiked tea), and gluwine are everywhere. The bellow of the crowd rolling up the mountain when I stood in the start house of a World Cup race felt like I was on the receiving end of a ferociously friendly and encouraging lion's roar. Imagine being a teenager and feeling the sounds, noise, and vibrations of thousands of strangers cheering for YOU, just you. The sensations penetrated my flesh and psyche. It was overwhelming, but captivating. I tuned out the distractions and did the best I could to execute a solid performance each time.

People of the European continent are diverse, however, and not every country there treats ski racing like it's the national pastime. Krista, Tanis, Gibson, Monique, Kristi, and I competed behind the iron curtain. The Europa Cup (a competition tour organized by the International Ski Federation, which takes place throughout Europe and is a level below the highest level of world competition, the World Cup) organizers scheduled a tour through several Eastern Bloc countries for both the men's and women's circuit. In March of 1989, roughly 125 competitors, officials, coaches, and other support people left the neutral country of Switzerland and headed east. The first stop was Ljubljana, Yugoslavia. Close by is the alpine village of Bled, a familiar locale for ski races. Many World Cup and Europa Cup events are held in the vicinity of Bled. We all had competed there before.

Next we flew to Sophia, Bulgaria, where Eastern Europe became more and more vivid the deeper we went. Krista cleared customs ahead of me. Shortly after, I made my way to the primitive customs cabin counter. The guard was ornamented with a heavy-duty machine gun, green uniform, hat, and military boots, and reached out for my passport. He looked at it, looked at me, looked again at my passport and outwardly became confused. I returned a look; stared at him innocently but with American confidence (or was it an eighteen-year-old girl's sassiness?). He left with my passport. I didn't like that. Then he huddled together with his comrades. I'm sure at this point I folded my arms in front of my chest. Time passed. I relaxed, sat on my luggage and waited out their confusion. The guard came back with a few of his friends . . . . and Krista. They stood us side by side, looked us over, flipped through our passports, talked among themselves in their language, stamped our passports, then sent us both through customs. Had they never seen twins before?

The hotel in Bulgaria was sparse, concrete. Rooms were comfortable but terribly smelly, like a sewer. The toilet, sink, and shower were part of the sleeping quarters. The hotel manager was exceptionally hospitable, though, gracious and overly accommodating. He served us flat Coca-Cola for breakfast and what I thought was chicken the rest of the time. Prior to departing the West, I knew meals in the Eastern Bloc could be a challenge, so

I had packed Swiss chocolate, Oreo cookies, and Quaker instant oatmeal.

Every road we traveled over in Bulgaria was paved with dirt. Skinny kids played soccer in the streets or on makeshift dirt fields. There was no grass. The training hill was about 150 feet wide and 250 feet long, with little to no vertical, and had a rope tow to transport us to the top. Certainly not a regulation training slope for the Europa Cup. But we made it work. The race hill was serviced by a modern quad lift that broke down often. I don't recall my race performance, which means I probably didn't perform very well.

Bulgaria, 1989 Europa Cup pre-race training.

From Sophia, we flew over the Black Sea to Tbilisi in Georgia, then still under Russian rule. Over the Black Sea, I thought we were going to die as the airplane shuddered, dove, and then climbed. Out of the window, I could see thick clouds; heavy weather had enveloped us. Our airplane was filled with athletes and staff from every country competing on the Europa Cup. Surely we won't die, I thought. There won't be anyone left to compete.

We arrived safely. The entire Europa Cup circuit caravanned to the Caucasus Mountains a few hours away. The busy, hectic, paved, city roads of Tbilisi eventually turned into dirt. We drove through a cold, flat, barren landscape dotted with poor, tiny communities. Few people roamed those parts. It reminded me of the places Tolstoy described in *Resurrection*. Up, up, and farther up we drove, finally reaching heaven. Nothing existed up there except state-of-the-art ski lifts and one hotel, Austrian style. It was a wonderful place to be. The only time clouds moved in was to dot the sky with a more beautiful setting. The hotel was luxurious, had a bowling alley and a movie theater. The hospitality was professional, first class.

Oddly, the Russian team didn't stay there. Supposedly they didn't have enough money.

A day before the downhill competition (which I was scheduled to compete in, but I'd convinced my coach that this downhill course was much too dangerous for me), our team doctor, Dr. Stone, invited Krista, Tanis, and me to go helicopter skiing with him. Our coaches suggested we refrain from skiing in order to ensure our health and top performance in the upcoming competitions. Minding our coaches, we went along only for the ride. The Russian pilot was skinny, dark-haired, friendly, and seemingly excited to be taking Americans up in his helicopter. Before loading us into the old, rickety Russian rotorcraft the pilot handed out several Russian military fur hats and jackets for us to wear. We lifted off, despite the fact that the helicopter appeared far from being in compliance with any modern-day regulations. Nonetheless we felt like we were starring in a Russian spy movie. The pilot ferried us over the white mountain peaks that stretched on for eternity. I peered out the windows in awe, truly beside myself. From then on, I would never tire of gazing out of a window at altitude. We landed in a long field of snow, dropped off Dr. Stone, watched him ski through the virgin communist snowfields, and then flew over the untouched (except for the American tracks) mountain to pick him up. Dr. Stone was exhausted with delight and we were charmed by his joy. Back at the hotel we bragged and bragged about the experience. To this day I have never been back up in a helicopter. Nothing has since compared.

About a week later, we left the Caucasus Mountains and headed back to Tbilisi. Unrest seemed to consume the city. The feeling was tense and a little alarming. People walked in groups, dressed in dark colors, and tried not to be noticeable, as though they were hiding themselves. No one seemed happy. A month after leaving Russia I saw rioting, fighting, and looting—basically the beginnings of a civil war—in Georgia's capital of Tbilisi on TV.

"Holy cow, I was just there!" I said to my parents.

On April 9, 1989, violent clashes broke out between troops and protesters on the main square in front of the Georgian government building in the heart of Tbilisi. It became known as the Tbilisi Massacre, which left twenty people dead, mainly young women.

The last stop on the tour was Jasna, Czechoslovakia. It was the Europa Cup finals, where the men's and women's circuits came together to close out the Europa Cup tour. Because of logistics, housing, hill space, community impact, sponsors, and event venue finances, ski resorts typically host single-gender events. So the combination of the men's and women's teams competing at the same venue was always lots of fun. We got to hang out and mingle with the guys, meet new people, and experience a change in human scenery, vibe, and atmosphere.

Jasna was much like eastern Austria, with a slight feel of suppression and gloom, but dominated by western culture and attitudes. The accommodations were pleasant, and the food was edible. I competed well, placing second in the giant slalom. I won a beautiful, thick, hand-blown crystal vase. Jasna is well known for its crystal.

US Ski Team, Jasna, Czechoslovakia, March 1989. Back row: Lex, Kristi, Dr. Stone, Tanis, Tim, me, Chris. Front row: Monique, Gibson, Krista, Kent. And the girl under the flags is the Austrian who beat me in the giant slalom.

In mid-March we left Eastern Europe and headed straight to Crested Butte, Colorado, for the US Nationals. My best result was a respectable ninth in the slalom. A long season was coming to a close, but not before an unusually late major international competition. We competed in our final (because of age) Junior World Championships. This event was unique in many ways. It was held in April, the final competition of the season. Krista and I would fly to Hawaii after the final event to rest and relax. But most importantly, the competition was held in the United States (seldom are the Junior Worlds held in the US), and in Alaska of all places! From Alyeska Ski Resort's skiable peak of twenty-five hundred feet I could see icy, frigid, Chickaloon Bay, just off the Gulf of Alaska, and far off in the distance was the Bering

Sea, which borders Russia. Rocky, snowcapped mountain peaks surrounded me at eye level. I was closer to the Arctic Circle than I had ever been in my life. Icebergs roamed the bay.

Reluctantly I competed in the downhill in order to be a potential medalist in the combined event, which at that time included slalom, giant slalom, and downhill. I placed eighteenth in the downhill (I was scared to death during the entire race, even on the flats), tenth in the super G, and failed to reach the finish line during the first run of the slalom. My final Junior Worlds at this point was a disappointment, more like an embarrassment to someone who'd been a bronze medalist two years prior. I brushed it off and figured Hawaii was only a few days away. Since there was a direct flight from Alaska, Krista and I had planned a season-ending trip to Maui. With nothing to lose, I was relaxed going into the championship's last event, the giant slalom—my favorite discipline. I was free of expectation and mentally already on an airplane headed to Hawaii. If everything can go wrong before a major competition, it did for me that day. Morning warm-up was a disaster. From the corner of my eye, I could see my coach shaking his head each time I failed to complete every training run. I didn't care. That training course will be nothing like the racecourse, I told myself. It was short, rutty, and the rhythm was awkward and jerky.

With ease and not a care in the world, I completed my first race run in second place behind Germany's Katja Seizinger. Krista was an epic failure, placing twelfth after the first run and a full second behind the winning time, an eternity in ski racing. Then, the top fifteen finishers in the first run would compete in reverse order for the second and final run. That meant Krista would be the third competitor down the racecourse, I would be the fourteenth competitor and Katja would be the fifteenth competitor. The combined times of the two runs determined the winner.

Upon entering the starting gate for my final run, I lost a boot buckle. No big deal, I thought. The start coach was panicking, seeking every means to replace it. I was in a zone: Whatever happens, happens. All I can do is my best. He got the buckle replaced with about sixty seconds to spare before I was required to exit the start gate and begin my race run. I thanked him and entered the start corral. I knew Krista had put in a blazing second run and was leading the race after her disappointing twelfth-place first-run result. Wow, that's spectacular and not an easy feat. And not one she would have executed without the encouragement from Dad during the break between runs.

"Krista, do you know how long one second is?"

"No," she said, in the depths of despair.

"It's the blink of an eye." Then he blinked his large, twinkling, blue eyes (which Krista and I inherited) directly in front of Krista's gloomy face.

Dad had ignited in her the fire she needed. The idea of one second being the blink of an eye gave Krista a whole new perspective on her current position and infused a courage that propelled her to the leader position of the Junior World Championships . . . until I crossed the finish line.

I stood in the start, quiet and calm but determined while I assessed the racecourse below, visualizing for one last moment the route I would take. The ten-second warning start beep echoed. I slid close to the edge of the start ramp. Then slowly, carefully planted my ski poles over the start wand and stood in an athletic position. The five-second warning beeps began. Beep, beep, beep. I extended my ankles, knees, and the small of my back as the strength of my triceps, lats, elbows, hands, wrists, and stomach muscles thrust me up and forward. My shoulders and hips exploded over the start wand and onto the racecourse. Next, the flex point of my ski boots tripped the wand that started the clock. The heavy, water-soaked, sharp crystals of spring snow popped from the tail of my skis into the air like a Fourth-of-July fireworks show from the abrupt explosion of takeoff. Out of the start, I pushed fiercely with one and only one goal in mind: Go as fast as you can, Kim. (Much like that day at Pico, Vermont, when I was a pint-size disaster.)

The snow on the race track was firm and slick, but forgiving. The sky was Alaskan blue. The air was warm, spring-like. Every turn was fun. The air hugged me tight and my long hair flowed behind me in freedom. I darted with supple fluidity from gate to gate, gaining speed from the effortless technique that came naturally. My ankles and hips initiated every new turn. Then my knees sank the rest of my joints into an angular, powerful, and dynamic position. I smoothly carved every turn while I swished past each gate like it wasn't there. After I reached the finish, I glanced up at the scoreboard. My body radiated electricity, my face was a sparkling, rosy red, my hair windblown, and my heartbeat was fast. The large digital scoreboard planted on the bank of the hill adjacent to the lower third of the racecourse read:

1. K. SCHMIDINGER USA 2.09.19
2. K. SCHMIDINGER USA 2.09.69

What? Who's leading this race? I was confused and breathing heavily. *Was I in first place, or was Krista?*

In the meantime, Katja completed her final run. Now the scoreboard read:

1. K. SCHMIDINGER USA 2.09.19
2. K. SCHMIDINGER USA 2.09.69
3. K. SEITZINGER BRD 2.09.96

Of course Krista and I both wanted to know the official result, but whatever the case, one of us was a gold medalist and the other a silver medalist. The order at this point was inconsequential. Krista and I were already celebrating. Throughout the confusion that everyone was experiencing, someone told us. The result couldn't have been any better—for me anyway. I was a world champion. And on that day, the best junior ski racer in the world. Krista was second. We were proving to be formidable competitors on the world stage. And on that winning day I felt an inner confidence, a calm that has never left me.

As a matter of fact, that 1989 group is still the most successful US Junior World Team on record. We won eight medals at Alyeska. Five went to the women's team. Julie Parisian won bronze in the super G (and finished fourth in the 1992 Olympics). Gibson Lafountaine, our teammate from Stratton Mountain School, won silver in the slalom. Krista won two silvers, one in the giant slalom and one in the combined. And I won gold in the giant slalom. The men took the other three medals—all gold. Tommy Moe won the super G and the combined (and became an Olympic gold and silver medalist in 1994), and Jeremy Nobis won the giant slalom. Our powerful team won more medals than any other nation competing. That's unheard of. Our achievements caught the attention of the New York Times, which ran an article by Janet Nelson entitled "Skiing: A 70s Youth Movement" on April 17, 1989.

I continued to perform strongly, enough to keep climbing the ladder. My Junior World gold medal had earned me the 1989 Ski Racing magazine Junior of the Year award. In 1990, I scored consistently on the Europa Cup, placed top five in three events at the US Nationals, snuck into the top thirty a few times on the World Cup, and won the overall North American super G title—enough to prove that I was World Cup and Olympic material. My world rankings in the spring placed me on the cusp of the A team. This year the A-team criteria was top thirty in the world in one event. My world ranking in super G was thirty-second. The criteria to be named to the B team was top one hundred in the world in three events. I was an accomplished three-event skier and well within the B-team criteria once again. I would remain a B team member, two spots away from the A team. Krista earned a solid position on the A team with her downhill and super G world rankings.

1990 US National Super G podium. Me, Kristi Terzian, Krista, Diann Roffe, Hilary Lindh.

An athlete doesn't reach the top levels of a winter sport without enduring the pains and rigors of off-season exercise. Summer dry-land training and physical testing in Park City and Salt Lake City was sometimes brutal. We ran up and down the concrete stadium bleachers over and over again at the University of Utah. We ran 440-yard and 50-yard sprints on the blazing-hot artificial turf. We were required to do knuckle push-ups, speed jumps, and quick feet on the rigid track surface, all in 107-degree weather, with few water breaks. Without warning I got a bloody nose once, probably from dehydration or overexertion. We spent hours in the gym lifting weights and working on speed, agility, balance, and stretching.

Physical testing was part of each July dry-land camp, and would be recorded and judged somehow by someone. Who? I don't really know. How it figured into determining each athlete's on-snow performance level was subjective. One by one, we performed 440- and 50-yard sprints, box jumps, high jump, bench press, squats, Cybex machine, flexibility measurements, and VO2 max.

VO2 max taught me how to purposely endure pain and move beyond it. This test assessed the ability to maximize heart-rate. Meaning how long crazy, obedient, dedicated girls could strenuously exercise on a treadmill or stationary bike at a heart-rate of 180 beats (more or less) per minute. A mask connected to a hose strung to a machine and covered our mouths. Breathing from our noses was restricted. The flow and efficiency of oxygen throughout our fit bodies was recorded and monitored. The higher the heartrate for a sustained period of time, the better! It was a fine line between superb physical fitness and death. I'm happy to report: no one died!

We even had our body fat measured and blood analyzed. Now that girls can be Navy SEALs most of us would have qualified. However, a few athletes found creative ways to skip summer dry-land camp. They just didn't show up. Some were sent home because they weren't in shape. Maybe they were the smart ones! It took two weeks for my muscles and heart and lungs to recover from those military-style boot camps.

Non-testing dry-land camps sometimes took place at the Olympic training center in Lake Placid, New York. Other times we went to San Diego, which was a real treat because it was an attractive location, and while we weren't tested, we still endured rigid daily training sessions.

Through thick and thin, this way of life still was exciting, adventurous and rewarding.

Some of the members of the US Women's Ski Team in the fall of 1988 at Winter Park, Colorado. Back row: Heidi (our childhood teammate from the Bousquet Ski Club in Pittsfield, MA), Kristin, Krista, Sue (non-US Ski Team Member), Adele, Gibson, me. Front row: Monique, Eva, Tanis, Sally.

CHAPTER FIVE
Not Again

Lying in a hospital bed, dressed in a thin hospital-issued gown, tubes strung up my nose, another protruding from my chest, with an IV stuck into the top of my hand, my body itched uncontrollably from the anesthesia. Before surgery the nurse had tried seven times, yes SEVEN times, to insert the IV needle into any vein in either of my arms. After her fourth prick and sliding the needle back and forth just under my skin's surface each time, desperate to puncture a vein, tears flooded my eyes and I nearly fainted. But I assured the nurse that I was okay and could handle the torture. I didn't want to be categorized as difficult or make her feel like she wasn't good at her job. Her persistent efforts to penetrate any of my uncooperative veins were proving futile. The veins in both arms kept collapsing. That's why the IV was eventually butterflied into the top of my hand. Not the most comfortable location for an IV, because each time I tried to move or sit up from my hospital bed, I used my hands, causing the needle to jam deeper into my flesh and rip open my skin. Oww. Try walking on crutches with an IV needle embedded in your hand. Every time I tried to move myself the needle ripped my skin and it stung; thinking about it right now, I cringe from the memory of that pain.

A scary-looking brace tightly wrapped and cuddled my numbed right knee. My left knee was numb too. Alvin, my brown stuffed bunny, was tucked under my covers beside me. He traveled everywhere with me—my constant companion along with a pillow when the ones provided by hotels or airlines didn't do the job. My room was filled with flowers sent by family, friends, and sponsors. The sun shone brightly through the wide windows while I admired the Vail ski slopes of Born Free and Bear Trail.

I severely injured my right knee training slalom in Saas Fee, Switzerland, on October 22, 1990. I didn't even fall. While making a turn to the left around a slalom gate, things just snapped and tore. I fell to the ground. Immediately it didn't seem so bad. My coach skied over to me, asked if I was okay. With my left leg I lifted myself up from the pristine, snow-covered training slope, took my skis off, limped to protect my right knee in a circle over the sparkling snowfield perched on top of the world, and felt a twinge of instability. Maybe I'm okay, I thought. He suggested I step back into my bindings. Without thinking and hoping my knee was fine, I powerfully stepped my injured leg into my binding. Shorter than the hundredths of seconds that separate winning from losing a ski race, my entire body collapsed to the ground. Whatever injury came from the initial incident was now compounded by that careless move.

Not again! Yup, again.

I was piggybacked from the 11,000-foot glacier on that beautiful day by one of the trainers and transported via the underground funicular, then by gondola to the picture-book village of Saas Fee. From there an electric car drove me to the hotel. My teammates and several coaches waited on me hand and foot. Their kindness and compassion didn't derail my constant crying, though.

The next day I went through the same basic transcontinental travel drill as I had four years before when I injured my left knee. The team put me on an airplane in Zurich. I traveled cramped in economy class, alone, halfway around the globe on crutches. My injured knee was secured in a metal-lined, oversized brace that was strapped from my ankle to my groin. My upper and lower leg felt disconnected, held together only by skin. Any ounce of pressure or movement caused my knee to collapse or buckle. My knee ached and throbbed continuously. I knew this injury was severe.

Vans to Vail picked me up in Denver and drove me to the DoubleTree Hotel in Vail, where a chocolate chip cookie rested on my bed pillow. I gobbled it up—hungry for the comfort of something sweet. The next morning at six a.m., Dr. Steadman's very nice surgical nurse, Shirley, picked me up and took me to the Steadman-Hawkins Clinic at the Vail Valley hospital. I was twenty years old, at the top of my game, full of energy, determination, and confidence. I was still naive enough to believe that obstacles could be jumped over, crawled under, or walked around. But I was a little more experienced than I had been when I had my first knee operation at sixteen, knowing that it wouldn't be simple or easy.

Dr. Steadman had moved his entire practice to the Vail Valley in Colorado. I think the hospital built a whole new wing just for him. My single room was modern and the view was spectacular. The Ritz couldn't have been more comfortable. That was the upside.

There was quite a bit of downside, though: this wasn't a clean, seemingly straightforward partial tear of my medial collateral ligament like last time. I had completely torn my anterior cruciate ligament (ACL) and meniscus cartilage, and partially torn my medial collateral ligament (MCL). I chipped my femur and strained my lateral collateral ligament (LCL).

The surgery was long. My knee was filleted. The knife cut a four-inch line from the top of my kneecap toward my tibia, and another four-inch slice was cut on the medial side. The surgeons left the centimeter round scar from my bicycle accident when I was a little girl alone. Total knee reconstruction involved grafting a thin strip from the center of my patella tendon, which was neatly snipped and manicured. It was then attached to my femur and upper tibia or fibula, I'm not sure which, with screws. Real metal screws. So the patella tendon graft is now my new ACL. The MCL was sewn back together. The meniscus cartilage was treated in a way that stimulated a natural healing process, a technique called micro fracture, which Dr. Steadman pioneered.

That afternoon following surgery I crutched my way to SPORT, the rehab center. I did very little on my own, though. A caring and tender therapist removed my brace and slowly bent my knee back and forth in the most minimal range of motion. Excruciating pain was an understatement. I held back tears. When the therapist moved on to the next patient, I cried inside. Bottling up the emotion retracted the water welling up in my eyes and dissipated the itching in my nose. I recovered from the physical exhaustion and mental management of pain just in time for the therapist's return. He delicately moved my knee back and forth a couple more times. The session wasn't long, because enduring physical knee movements a few short hours after reconstructive surgery isn't easily tolerated. He gently taught me how to remove and reassemble my brace. That's about all we covered that day. I crutched back to my hospital room. A nurse helped me cozy back into my bed and rehooked the medical equipment. My injured knee neatly rested in a constantly moving ice machine. When she left, I cried. So did Alvin, my stuffed bunny.

A very, very, very tough road lay ahead, mentally, physically, and psychologically. I had no idea!

Six weeks on crutches, non-weight-bearing, and a limited range of motion were the first hurdles to overcome. Those days were rough. Sleeping was uncomfortable and often painful. Showering was a hassle. Changing the surgical dressing was a long and gentle process. I often caressed and massaged my naked, numb, swollen and useless knee, believing whole-heartedly that it could feel my compassion and perhaps heal a little quicker. The muscles surrounding my broken and deformed knee were atrophied, no longer the strong, healthy composed tissues they had always been. Everything I did was slow. My pathetic joint dictated everything I did and everything I didn't do.

Simply bending and straightening ten degrees was a ferocious task. Not only was my knee tightly sewn and stitched together, but scar tissue, blood and whatever else had built up in there made for a cruel loosening process.

Time and consistent therapy eased the torturous physical pain. In six weeks, I was walking with one crutch. My stability wasn't 100 percent, my patella tendon remained sore, and the four-inch slits in my skin stayed numb for about a year. Swelling slowly deflated, but never entirely. And my LCL and carved-up patella tendon found their way back to health over the course of the rehab period.

Prior to my knee injury, Krista and I had acquired a new sponsor, Volkl skis, located in Banner Elk, North Carolina. Volkl USA was co-owned by Gunther Jochl and his partner, Dale Stancil. Gunther was also the general manager of Sugar Mountain Resort, Inc., and Dale was the owner. *What? There's snow in North Carolina? Do they even have mountains? Surely they don't know how to ski down there.* My Yankee arrogance spoke loud and clear. Believe me, Yankees can be overly proud and pompous, even when we're clueless. Krista and I were invited to the annual Volkl USA spring meeting in Banner Elk, where we were introduced to the management and sales teams. I was amazed at the area's beauty and stunned to see the steep, rugged Appalachian Mountains.

Since I had inconveniently blown out my knee six months

after signing with a new ski sponsor, for the first time in my life I had the freedom and opportunity to do whatever I wanted for the following six months, as long as rehab was my priority. Appalachian State University (ASU) was near Sugar Mountain and a perfect diversion to knowing that there was a competition season I wouldn't participate in for the first time since I was six years old. And living full-time at home with my parents with nothing to do at the age of twenty was not an appealing option. I had always thrived on academics when I had the time, so I enrolled in the spring semester at ASU and spent time at Sugar Mountain Ski Resort, and even got a part-time job working with the Sugar Mountain ski club.

College was right up my alley and a fruitful distraction to days that otherwise had been consumed with rigid training, competition, or traveling. Philosophy class gave me a headache, though. It's exponential, like infinity. No solution. I don't exist like that. My life has paths, routes that reach for goals and end with accomplishment or failure. Philosophy is ambiguous, intangible. History was a little mind-boggling as well, because I was required to retain a wealth of information, and then regurgitate it on exam day. There wasn't much learning there, just memorization. I don't memorize things. I think them through, then execute intuitively. Advanced German was easy, obviously, and freshman algebra and trigonometry was interesting and kept my attention. Which doesn't mean I necessarily did well, but it was stimulating. I relished the academic challenge, most of the time.

The behavior of Southerners and their culture was different. Rebel flags, southern slang, a slow pace, numerous and undefined Christian denominations, and southern hospitality were a big change from only American flags, a fast pace, defined religion, superficial cynicism, and the tough character of New Englanders. Naturally, it took a little getting used to, particularly the heavy accents and unreserved doses of Christianity. Sooner rather than later, though, I fit right in and appreciated the lifestyle and culture. Rehab was my priority, and school flowed neatly around it.

In late February, Dr. Steadman and I decided to scope my left knee (not the one that was just reconstructed) to remove plica (an injury to the knee can cause thickening or scarring to the plica tissue) and scar tissue—sort of a clean-up from the wear and tear of a life full of demanding athletics and the surgery four years before. It was a good thing, but every time I went under the knife, it took a toll on my body.

I missed skiing, competing, and equally important: winning. Trivial accomplishments like walking without crutches, having a range of motion to ride a bicycle, bending to kneel, a night's sleep without pain or throbbing, showering without having to cover my knee with plastic, and driving a car were some of the everyday activities I took for granted prior to reconstructive knee surgery. Reaching each mundane benchmark inspired the effort to work hard toward the next goal.

The competition season went on without me, as does everything in life if you don't participate. Krista was making her mark on the World Cup competing all over Europe, the United States, and Japan. I was happy and proud when she did well, and irritated but compassionate when she didn't. Her performance was my performance. That's the way we operated. When one wins, we both win. When one fails we pull the other one up. Another twin thing.

Early March was a real turning point in my rehabilitation. My knee grew stronger and more powerful. It actually looked like a real knee with a kneecap and bones. Muscles even began to emerge. Another month and I'd be on snow. Yahoo! It was all downhill from here!

I flew to Colorado where, on April 4, Dr. Steadman gave me the go-ahead to get back on snow. I free skied and free skied all day long until the lifties in Vail said, "Sorry, we're closed for the day."

I was so excited to be on the snow, blowing some arcs and ripping it up. I was smiling from ear to ear. It was exhilarating. I couldn't wait for the next day. *If only skiing could be like this all the time.*

I finished up my semester at ASU and then in June I matriculated back into the team's schedule and routine, but with the B Team. It was a blow and wore on me psychologically. My teammates since I was fifteen years old were racing World Cup. Plus all of my summer and fall preparation prior to my injury was with the A-team squad. *We* were the A Team now—only, the *we* no longer included *me*. I felt left behind, with even more challenging obstacles to clear.

Throughout the summer but in between summer training camps, Krista and I had enrolled in summer classes at ASU. We enjoyed North Carolina and had begun searching for a rental property to purchase. We had considered investing in property in the Vail Valley in Colorado, but that was unrealistic since it was so far away and so much more expensive. We looked around our hometown area but didn't find a quality property within our price range or that was seasonally rentable. Several properties in North Carolina fit our criteria, and college during the summer semesters was just a short drive away. That fall with the earnings from the successes in our skiing careers, we bought a small house on Sugar Mountain as an investment and a place to crash when we weren't on the road. We called it "the Treehouse," because it sat up high on a steep bank and tree branches hovered close, touching the windows and siding. We rented out the property during the winter months to help offset the mortgage and began spending our downtime in North Carolina.

Just do your best, Kim. It'll all work out. Stay confident, I told myself.

Not only was it a psychological struggle from then on, but it was a physical and mental fight too. Throughout the 1991 summer and fall training camps, I was moved back and forth from the B team to the A team. My knees were always sore and fatigued. I experienced some productive and inspiring training sessions, and other times it was grim and counterproductive. I was a car on a roller coaster moving up and down. One good day, two bad days. I loved skiing, and then I couldn't wait to get a break.

Fritz, my coach back at Stratton Mountain School, was now the US Women's A team technical head coach. That's where I should have been but wasn't. I was still with the B team. He and the A-team girls were loading up the van on their way to training one October day at Beaver Creek.

"Kim, I'm saving a seat for you," he said.

I looked him in the eye and thought, *I know you are. If only I can get there.*

With a grimace on my face and the hope he meant to communicate easing into my spirit, my heart sank. I walked away, disappointed that I wasn't there already.

Fritz went on to lead several successful US Women's Teams and lead the Austrian Men to some of their most successful years in history. He is revered and well respected in the world of international alpine skiing.

Unpredictably, since I believed with every strand of my being that I would be back better and stronger than before, my life got worse once the competition season began. Mentally insecure and physically apprehensive, I couldn't finish races. I'd hook a gate, lose my balance or timing, cross my tips, catch or lose an edge, find a snow snake (an unexplained reason for failure), lean in, or make any number of mistakes that forced a disqualification. When I did reach the finish line, I was seconds behind those I'd usually beaten with my eyes closed. Okay, that's an exaggeration, but that's what it felt like. In December, I raced Nor-Ams. From January to March, I was back on the Europa Cup and competed in a few World Cups.

Me, competing in a Nor-Am on Stratton Mountain in Vermont 1991 or 1992. Photo credit Hubert Schriebl.

My performance in the World Cup in Tigne, France, was embarrassing. Although I competed like a regional racer instead a world-class pro, I got to absorb the sun and its glow rising over the Alps—stunning! At seven a.m. I was half asleep, riding the T-bar, alone with my competition skis propped over my shoulder, en route to prerace training and course inspection. It was a clear, crisp, dark, frigid morning. My breath nearly froze every t..... exhaled. The stars and the moon were setting behind me while a slim, horizontal line of twinkling orange began to peek up and over the mountain bank I was about to crest. An imposing perfect fireball of brilliant sparkling red and orange climbed closer and closer right before my eyes. For a brief moment, the sun engulfed my entire existence. Nothing else was visible, not even peripherally. Then the gentle but striking and mighty sun grew smaller and smaller as it rose to light and warm the European continent. A new day never fails. And I realized, like I had so many times in the past, that something grander, more powerful than humans would always be in charge.

For me, life continued on that roller coaster. Krista and several of my teammates were off to the Olympics in Albertville. For Krista, the 1992 Olympics in Albertville, France, was a spectacular double-edged sword experience. She placed twelfth in the downhill competition and eleventh in the combined event, now a blend of the downhill and slalom disciplines. Number twelve out of the combined downhill event start house, she excelled, making beautiful, long, high-speed, sweeping turns over steep terrain. Each interval split time brought her closer and closer to the first-place position. She glided with ease and suppleness over the flats, and flew dynamically over the first two jumps. Reaching a speed of 75 mph, she skied wide, dramatically rubbing the course's manmade padded wall. The spectators held their breath in fear of a pending nasty crash as they watched the Jumbotron from the finish line. But Krista's daredevil athleticism seamlessly turned the potential disaster into a second-place finish, just five-tenths of a second behind the powerhouse Austrian Petra Kronberger. The finish crowd roared with excitement as a young underdog, an American, was poised for an Olympic medal. That morning she received a fax from tennis star Martina Navratilova saying, "Show them how good you are!" That she did. But a poor slalom performance the next day ratcheted her back to an overall eleventh-place finish in the combined. Mom and Dad were there to watch. Beloit Company, Dad's employer, covered their expenses.

After the 1992 Olympics, our little town put together a homecoming celebration for Krista. Just off exit two of the Massachusetts Turnpike stood a Department of Transportation sign saying "Welcome home, Krista, 1992 Olympian." Main Street was packed with people of every age from all over Berkshire County. A fire engine drove us (I got a hero's welcome too) through the cheering crowd via Main Street to the Greenock Country Club, where the celebration took place.

"Krista, Krista, you have a phone call," someone informed her, then swooshed her back to a private room.

When she came out, she told me, "Kim, that was Senator Ted Kennedy congratulating me on my performance and thanking me for representing the United States."

"Wow, that's cool," I said.

But a four-term Massachusetts Republican senator (Yes, Republicans exist in Massachusetts, but just barely!) played a more supportive, long-lasting role in Krista's career. Senator Jack Fitzpatrick and his wife Jane took Krista under their wing, sponsoring her financially and welcoming her into the circles and places of the elite and exceptional. The Senator, as he liked to be called, was a teddy bear of a man, remarkably witty, and with a dry sense of humor. He created laughter wherever he went. Jane, whom most people called Mrs. Fitz, was the engine. She was a no-nonsense lady who asked direct and penetrating questions. Never shy, always engaging, and funny as well.

Mr. and Mrs. Fitz were the founders of Country Curtains,

the nation's first mail-order curtain company, which began at their dining room table in the 1950s. They energized and rebuilt the Red Lion Inn in Stockbridge, Massachusetts. Today, it remains the emblematic heart and soul of the Berkshires. They were friends with Norman Rockwell, and even posed for one of his paintings in 1964. They were the driving force behind Tanglewood, the Boston Symphony Orchestra's summer home in Lenox. Equally important, they were dedicated philanthropists supporting the arts, education, endless causes, and many exceptional people from Western Massachusetts, like Krista.

The Senator and Mrs. Fitz gave Mom and Dad an all-expenses-paid trip to Krista's second appearance in the 1994 Olympics in Lillehammer, Norway, where Krista placed twenty-seventh in the downhill competition.

Remember that bronze medalist in the 1989 Junior World Championships giant slalom, Katja Seizinger, a fellow competitor from our youth? Well, she went on to become a superstar. She won three Olympic gold and two bronze medals, plus eleven World Cup season titles. While training in June of 1998 she injured both knees, sat out the entire 1999 season, and then retired in April.

Clearly everyone's journey was filled with fun and hardship, success and failure.

The junior ranks were truly a reflection of potential and indicated how one should perform at the World Cup, World Championship, and Olympic levels. Not everyone reached their potential. I'm one of them. Many had reputable and outstanding careers. Few became champions. After all, there's only one winner. But what we all had in common was the road. It was wide and went in the same direction for everyone. Along that path were injuries, varying levels of support, attitude, character, mental strength, and so many other determining variables.

Winning is easy when you work hard and are anointed with talent, but you can never predict what will get in the way or catapult you ahead along your journey to be the best.

During the Albertville Olympics, I left Europe and went back to the States because I hadn't qualified. In alpine skiing, four athletes per discipline from each country earn the privilege to compete in the Olympics. I trained with a US Ski Team coach I had worked with off and on over the years. He brought out the best in me, and I could relate to his teaching strategy. It seemed I was getting my groove back. Or so I thought.

Two weeks later, I headed back to competition, it turned out that time and training hadn't healed any of my visible or invisible wounds or made me any better. Nothing had changed since December, except that I had learned that I should at least try to handle my failures gracefully, without a tantrum or severely putting myself down. I continued to second-guess myself, and competed tentatively. I was insecure, fearful—but of what? I searched endlessly for solutions. Were my challenges mental, psychological, physical, a combination of all three? I was lost in every way.

Quietly walking away seemed like the most dignified of any route. The thought of retiring snuck up on me every now and then. I wasn't ready for that, didn't want to go there. After all, I was just shy of twenty-two years old. I wanted to achieve my goals, not just keep reaching for them. I kept debating with myself about my predicament, until I finally concluded that I was a ski racer and a good one.

Keep fighting, Kim. Things will turn around, I told myself over and over again.

I finished the season on the B Team once again. But I was worn out, hollow. I felt like quitting. Mom and Krista supported my decision no matter what it was, but Dad encouraged me to take a year off, rest my body, and resume the following season. The light at the end of the tunnel was dark. I decided to quit. The decision was liberating, but daunting, too. *What do I do, where do I go?* Life had always had a path for me, sometimes a hard one, but the direction was clear. Now I felt unsettled, insecure, like a girl with a million options but no skills, no experience, no knowledge, nor any confidence to make a choice. I was no longer eligible to compete for a university's ski team, plus why would I ski race any longer? It physically hurt. I didn't have a college degree, so I couldn't jump into employment that would financially support me.

So I loaded up my used four-wheel drive Toyota Tercel and moved to North Carolina. Just about everything I owned was stuffed and jammed into my silver-gray station wagon. The twelve-hour drive was calming, relaxing, and exciting, too! I was free. A brand-new world lay ahead. I couldn't wait.

I had considered going back to Appalachian State University but I wanted a fresh start, a new location, away from skiing. The Director of Admissions at ASU helped me transfer to the University of North Carolina at Greensboro. I arrived in Winston-Salem that evening to a barren, urban, chicken-coop apartment, which a friend had arranged for me.

Ab-so-lutely NOT, I thought. *There is no way I am living here. What have I done? I hate it here.* I began crying. The sorry-for-yourself kind of cry. Not a physically painful or heartache cry. A tender, desperate, *I'm stuck* cry!

Cars were zooming by the apartment complex one after the other along the busy four-lane highway. There was no grass, and a parking lot surrounded my new prison. An old lady dressed in her nightgown and slippers, cigarette hanging from her mouth, who seemed to do nothing but spy on her neighbors, appeared to be my neighbor.

But it was too late to ditch the place. I slept overnight, crying on and off while I figured out my next move. At the break of dawn, I got back into my car and drove to Sugar Mountain, where I knew that grass, trees, mountains, chirping birds, happy squirrels, roaming turkeys, a family of deer freely grazing, even the possibility of a bear sighting, and a familiar existence awaited. The two-hour drive was plenty of time for my swollen eyes and puffy face to recover from the intermittent bouts of crying. Since my treehouse was rented, I stayed at a friend's vacant mountain house for a few days trying to figure out my life. Then I got in my car and drove back to Massachusetts.

Within a few days I was headed back to the life I knew and what I was supposed to be good at: ski racing. The team was skeptical and only halfheartedly supported me, but the decision to return made me comfortable and gave me purpose again. Don't get me wrong: I was uncertain, too. It's not a typical route for many athletes, but I continued to train hard on and off the snow throughout the summer and fall of 1992. My training was modified to accommodate my constantly sore and tired knees, both of which had been through the wringer. My left knee underwent surgery when I was sixteen and my right knee when I was twenty. Both knees had maintenance surgeries when I was twenty-one. There were more surgeries on my right knee, but honestly, I've lost count. I substituted high-impact with low-impact conditioning. So instead of sprints on a track, I did sprints on rollerblades or a bicycle, for example. Ultimately, I needed a strategy that would condition my entire body with minimal stress on my joints while focusing on ski-specific muscles. At my expense, I spent several weeks at the Burdenko Water and Sports Therapy Institute, just outside of Boston.

My mom's mom, Momsie, let me stay with her in Beverly, just north of Boston, while I trained with Igor Burdenko. Momsie was an elegant but stern lady with seven kids, six of them girls and the last one a boy. Lipstick was probably all she had time for. It made her look delicate, not like the tough, strong lady she was. She always tucked her lipstick in her purse. Not often, but once in a while when I was a little girl, I would catch her in front of the mirror, gracefully coloring her lips. When she caught me shyly admiring her process, in her thick, old-fashioned Boston accent she said, "Kimmie, come ova here," and she gently but with strength cupped my chin with her fingers and affectionately colored in my lips. Then shooed me away saying, "and don't tell yor motha."

I liked that. I walked around the house feeling pretty, and of course didn't tell Mom.

Three to four days a week, Igor the Russian trainer ran me through a stringent, progressive water exercise routine, which was complemented by a low-impact land strength exercise routine. The philosophy is that the hydrostatic and hydrodynamic properties of water provide an optimal environment for safe and effective therapy and conditioning. With little or no weight-bearing necessary in the water, an injury and the body around it is able to heal and strengthen stress-free. The method undoubtedly relieved some of the physical challenges I was up against. It provided powerful and quick results.

By the start of the competition season, I was physically tired and worn out, but mentally eager to put the most horrible season behind me, and prove I could come back.

When I got back on the road, I tried to incorporate the water therapy, conditioning and training whenever possible. However, pulling a pool out of my suitcase was impossible, and finding one in European mountain villages wasn't easy either. If I did find a public pool, access was often expensive. Aching and soreness in both knees consumed me physically. Hanging my right leg from the chairlift was painful. The grafted patella tendon was creating a misalignment in the flow of my kneecap over the knee joint, or something like that. Regardless, it caused pain. Not what an athlete needs just prior to every training run or competition. Enduring the hardships and physical pain, I pushed through every domestic and international competition for three months with little to no success.

So, I went back to Colorado and saw Dr. Steadman again. He recommended specific exercises and taping my knee to align the kneecap. I was open to every recommendation, traditional and nontraditional, anything!

The physical requirements of ski racing, cold temperatures, high altitude, torqueing and angular positions are demanding enough on healthy and fit joints. But they were overwhelming to my already compromised knees. The taping, unfortunately, didn't relieve my discomfort.

After many non-invasive efforts, Dr. Steadman and I agreed to scope *both* knees again. Back under the knife I went. He cleaned and tightened my knee joints; made them fresh and new once more. The hospital was delightful, refreshing—a needed break. But only for a short time. I got bored and impatient. Since I wouldn't be released from the hospital for another day, I decided to escape.

That late winter day was warm and sunny. I unplugged the wires attached to my body then put on a pair of shorts and a sweatshirt. Butterfly bandages tightly held all eight (four per knee) orthoscopic incisions together. *Both* my knees were wrapped with Ace bandages. Gauze pads soaked up any oozing blood. I walked stiffly like a robot down the hallway to the elevators, smiling nicely at each nurse I passed.

"I'm just riding the elevators for fun. Maybe detour to the newborn baby floor," I told them.

They smiled back.

Down the elevator I went to the first floor, through the main lobby, and through the automatic doors. I was out! Tentatively, I walked to the bus stop and waited for the public bus. Once it arrived, I eked my way up the stairs. Then I methodically walked down the aisle of the bus, holding firmly to each seat, and found a place to sit. The bus driver was probably thinking—*Oh my God: I just picked this girl up at the hospital bus stop, she has two bandaged knees that barely bend, an IV needle in her hand, a hospital ID around her wrist, and she looks a little shaky. I hope she's going to be okay.*

I rode to the Häagen-Dazs store and cautiously got off the bus, which had stopped directly in front of the ice cream shop. I bought myself a coffee milkshake, got back on the bus, and contently slurped it down. I was happy.

Upon returning, the bus let me off directly in front of the hospital. I sat on the bus stop bench and found solace in the beautiful spring-like weather, peacefully. Then I casually snuck back into the hospital. No one ever was the wiser—not even Dr. Steadman.

I returned to competition two weeks later. This time the team put me on the domestic FIS/NCAA Division I competition circuit, headed up by an understanding and compassionate female US Ski Team coach. I won six races in a row, every competition I had entered, handily. It felt good. I knew it was levels below where I needed to be. Nonetheless, I was encouraged, and my coaches seemed to have a renewed confidence in me. Still, it wasn't easy to win at any level, especially under the pressure of expectation and with failure surrounding my every effort.

I met back up with the A team at the US Nationals in Winter Park, Colorado. Disaster. I failed to complete the giant slalom and performed horribly slowly in the super G.

To make my experience worse, the officials chose me for their random drug test.

"For real? I'm clearly not even a contender and you're drug-testing me? Do I look like a girl who takes drugs?" I asked irreverently. Escorted by an official, off I went to the drug-testing headquarters near the finish line. I peed in a cup and passed the drug test. Yay! There wasn't any question in my mind about what the results would be, but it satisfied the rules patrol.

The next day I finished in the top ten of the slalom. Not impressive, but not catastrophic either.

My performance that weekend clinched the team's decision to offer me an ultimatum: "Kim, the B Team is going to Asia in a few days. We're not taking you. You can train on your own over the summer and next season work yourself back onto the team," a US Ski Team coach told me nonchalantly, without compassion.

That hurt. But not more than the struggle I'd endured over the previous two and a half years. I sat for a few moments and sighed deeply while comprehending what he'd just said. By now I was almost twenty-three years old. Everything I had experienced and achieved in life didn't matter anymore. I was at the lowest point of existence; not just physically, but mentally and psychologically, too. I was broken.

Officially I was still a qualified B team member, but for some reason that didn't matter to the team.

I looked at him and without emotion replied, "Okay."

What else could I say? The road he presented now looked even harder than the road I'd just painfully traveled. My words didn't matter, just wasted energy.

I was disposable. I got up and walked away. It was time to move on.

That decision meant Krista and I would now truly be living separate lives. She continued the life of a world class ski racer, reaching a top-fifteen world ranking in downhill, that crazy discipline where you lunge yourself out of the starting gate, down fifty-degree-grade, icy ski slopes, with the sole intention of reaching speeds of 70+ mph in a speed suit, with only a helmet for protection. She competed in two World Championships, two Olympics, and was a guest in the White House. Her ski racing career concluded in 1997, four years after mine ended.

CHAPTER SIX
Civilian Life

FREEDOM! (Sing it like George Michael.) That's how I felt—FREE. I now had a chance to discover a world I'd never known, a life without the physical demands, the psychological games, the stress of personal expectation, the changing criteria, the times, and the numbers of competition. I was excited about gaining a different perspective, meeting new people, and making decisions that were my own. My stint with the US Ski Team was over. No more mandatory daily workouts, sore knees, trips to the hospital, or heartless coaches trampling all over my character. I wasn't going to be a walking billboard for sponsors I had no connection to, or live in that "Me, Me" competitive world anymore! Plus, by this time I hated skiing.

I reenrolled in Appalachian State University, where I already had a semester's worth of credit.

Sugar Mountain became my home, although I'd never intended it to be.

To ensure financial security and true independence, I happily juggled college and a job as Sugar Mountain Ski Resort's special events director. I wasn't a typical college girl. Since I'd lived and traveled with people since the eighth grade, that lifestyle didn't suit me anymore. I preferred and needed to spend my nonacademic hours earning a living. Plus, my classmates were two to five years younger than I was. I drove twenty minutes back and forth to campus five days a week, immersed in learning, and then escaped back to the wonderful world of reality: work. I thrived at work. Loved it. For an entire year I was in awe every Friday when I held my very own modest paycheck. I lived frugally in the Treehouse and saved everything I could.

Several months into civilian life, I received a letter from the US Ski Team. *Oh wow! A letter from the US Ski Team. I wonder what it says?* It notified me that my health insurance was canceled. I threw it in the trash. *Really? A little late on that one and that's all you've got to say? What kind of heartless, out-of-touch people make up the US Ski Team management anyway?* I thought. Good thing my job provided insurance.

Better letters, but unexpected, came from Appalachian State University. They informed me that I'd made the dean's list, and another one came letting me know I was on the chancellor's list. I wasn't ultrasmart or anything (Believe me, my SAT scores told me that! I never did take them again after my first attempt in Colorado.), just disciplined, and I was always surprised when I achieved anything academically noteworthy.

After the required four semesters of general undergraduate courses, I dove into the college of business. I have no idea why. It was comfortable, and I liked being there. Statistics was a real bear, though. Especially since I was a real-life, failed statistic. Back when I was ski racing, one of the many US Ski Team coaches liked to run the numbers. Well . . . his numbers said that Krista and I statistically were destined to be champions. He used real data: our actual results. Unfortunately, statistics neglected to consider the most important of immeasurable variables: the human factor.

My environment, my pain, my injuries and my state of mind were all immeasurable to the conventional platform of statistics, therefore missing key variables in neatly constructed statistical formulas. Standard deviation, probability, or whatever variable stats injects into its recipe is supposed to cover the unknown? Yeah, right. It doesn't. Typical of statistics!

I passed statistics with a C+, even though my first test grade was a fifty-eight. *FIFTY-EIGHT?* That was a stunner.

I knew I wouldn't do well. But when I walked up to the list of grades posted outside the professor's door and saw 58 percent across from my social security number, I nearly died. No need to feel shame, because the social security number was supposed to keep grades private. Regardless, I was sure my classmates were wondering which lame-brain got a fifty-eight!

Macro-economics and food science weren't my best subjects either. I squeaked by with Cs. But I sailed through the rest of the required business-school classes with As and Bs. I jumped, weaved, and bobbed through the academic institution's red tape in order to avoid the required general education PE class. I just didn't see the point in wasting time participating in low-level athletics! After all, I was a world-class athlete. It was like putting a genius in freshman math class. You just don't do that.

So I filled out paperwork, met with the chair of the Health, Leisure, and Exercise Science Department, filled out more paperwork, waited, and stood my ground until I finally got a waiver. They let me take ballet to fulfill the requirement, which was a big deal because ballet wasn't considered a Health, Leisure, and Exercise Science class. My sore knees seemed to appreciate the slow, methodical, stretching of an entry-level ballet class. I got an A.

Challenging the system proved fruitful. Appalachian State University came through for me, demonstrating that a rigid, unbending institution can indeed exercise its flexibility and operate not only for the masses, but also for the exception of individualism.

I graduated in 1997 with a bachelor of science degree in business administration. I toyed with the idea of pursuing an

MBA. But then I realized I'd been a productive and responsible human being since the age of twelve. I'm gonna take a break, I decided. That "break" turned my job at Sugar Mountain Resort into genuine full-time employment. I got a pay raise, had my own office that looked out onto the ski slopes, a telephone, a computer, and approached it all with an ambition that wouldn't take no for an answer.

While I was still in college and long before my job at Sugar Mountain Resort became permanent full-time employment, I had researched and implemented new events, reinstated shelved ones, and supported what was then the taboo sport of snowboarding. I had no idea that many ski area operators throughout the country considered snowboarding a dangerous addition to winter sports. Some even outlawed it, citing liability issues. That was ludicrous to me. A handful of girls I had competed with while on the US Ski Team had switched over to snowboarding, laying the foundation for it to become a legitimate sport and a positive addition to the snow sports industry.

I still didn't like to ski much, but stayed involved by coaching the Sugar Mountain Ski Club and introducing an adult preseason ski clinic. I invited some of my former US Ski Team teammates to mentor and instruct the group of adult ski racers. Participants from all over the southeast came for my three-day intensive on-snow training camp. Twenty years later, it's still going strong.

Every now and then I skied with Gunther. Remember Gunther, the general manager of Sugar Mountain Ski Resort and the owner of Volkl USA, my equipment sponsor? He's the one who gave me my first real job after the Ski Team graciously offered me that ultimatum. He'd nagged me with the notion that I DO love skiing, trying to convince me that it would just take time to find the thrill again. Yet I still didn't find it rewarding. Plus, now I had to share the slopes with people—imagine that:

regular people, recreational skiers, paying customers! How inconvenient. When you're a Ski Team member, entire slopes around the world at first-class resorts like Vail, Aspen, Tigne, St. Moritz, Courcheval, Madonna di Campiglio, Schladming, Grindelwald, Chamonix (and the list goes on) are closed to the public, reserved just for the team. Tiny community-managed jewels scattered within the mountains of the world rolled out the red carpet for national alpine teams too. Enlisting into civilian life had few drawbacks, but sharing the slopes and skiing with large crowds was one of them.

My first summer on the job at Sugar was too slow for me. So I initiated a summer program: building a network of mountain-biking and hiking trails all by myself. I took the company four-wheeler, a load of tools, and headed for the woods. I cleared abandoned horse trails, built new trails from scratch, and marked the system with 4x4 posts that I'd found on overgrown and undeveloped lots scattered throughout the mountain. The posts were property markers left over from the original plotting of Sugar Mountain back in the late sixties.

The following summer, I took a shot in the dark and proposed that Sugar Mountain Resort host National Off Road Mountain Biking Association (NORBA) competitions. At the first event, 150 mountain bikers showed up to compete in torrential, unrelenting rain and high winds. I competed too. I was covered from head to toe in mud. My face was caked and drenched with water and slimy dirt. Every other participant looked just like me. The grassroots event turned into a two-day affair, growing bigger and bigger each year. A few summers later I proposed weekend chairlift rides from Sugar's 4,100-foot base to its 5,300-foot summit for hikers, bikers, and anyone wanting to experience the fun. It provided a few part-time jobs and some extra cash flow for the ski area.

Me, post-NORBA race, 1994. I won my class.

And throughout all this, I was finding me! I even found out things I didn't know about myself. Like the tenacity that took over when I went for a mountain bike ride past the waterfall bridge along Shawneehaw Road in the town of Banner Elk. Out of nowhere, a small, dilapidated, pickup truck with a rebel flag, Tennessee tags, and a shotgun hanging in the back window passed me, and nearly ran me off the road.

A voice yelled, "Get off the road you f—ing whore."

I was startled. But not intimidated in the least. *What did he just call me? An effing whore! I am NOT an effing whore. Who does he think he is, calling me that?* I was livid and talking to myself. *He can't just go around yelling profanity out his truck window while attempting to run me off the road. I could have*

been killed. Splat, dead, third-degree murder because of his juve-
nile behavior! I thought.

No way. I am not taking that. This road is just as much mine
as it is his. I pay North Carolina taxes.

My mind was made up.

About 400 yards ahead was Banner Elk's only traffic light.
Faster than the Tasmanian Devil, I pedaled my heart out to catch
that truck. All the while begging the stoplight gods to ensure the
light remained red so I could have a word with those punks.

"It's red. Yes, the traffic light is red! The truck is first in line.
Please stay red. Please, please, please. Faster Kim, pedal faster," I
said over and over again, cheering myself on. "I got 'im!" Out of
breath, I whispered my excessive relief.

The truck's passenger side window was rolled down. With
sweat dripping down my beet-red face and my heart thumping
out of my chest, I laid my left hand on the passenger-side door
and carefully balanced on my bike as I caught my breath. I
turned my head toward the young, skinny, alarmed boy and
calmly, with raised eyebrows, I asked, "What did you say to me?"

"Uhhh . . . uh. He said it," the coward replied, pointing to his
equally skinny friend in the driver's seat.

I leaned in a little closer, and with more domineering authority
I looked at the driver and asked again, "What did YOU say to me?"

Squirming, a little scared—probably shaking in his boots—
the driver stuttered, "Ah, I, I didn't say anything."

"That's what I thought. Don't ever do that again," I scolded
like a well-seasoned mother, which I wasn't, yet.

The light turned green. The driver hit the gas pedal as though
he and his friend were fleeing the scene of a bank robbery. The
truck turned left toward Tennessee, leaving me high and dry. But
I have good balance and am agile on a bike. I remained balanced
and pedaled in the opposite direction.

"Where are the police when a girl needs 'em?" I asked, disgusted.

I wish I was packing some iron! . . . Without bullets of course, 'cause I surely would have pulled my Smith and Wesson .38 Special, scared 'em half to death, and made a citizen's arrest. Tennessee punks! I thought. (I really do have a .38 Special.)

They got the message, Kim. Don't worry, said the soothing, reasonable voice in my head.

My life, like everyone's, has been populated by a cast of characters—from lunatics (like those young Tennessee punks) to some truly endearing people. They come and go, but some have stayed constant. One of those constants is my soul mate, Gunther. The first time I met Gunther, he listened as though what I said mattered. His gentleness and sincerity made an impression on me. He had freckles and pretty blue eyes. He wore a brown suit that fit snugly to his stocky, buttery frame. He was professional and admired young people chasing the dream to become champion ski racers. After all, he was one himself back in the day.

Over time, we became fast friends, realizing we had a lot in common and enjoyed each other's company. It's wonderful when a friendship blossoms into a love affair. He fell in love with me first. Naturally, he'll deny that. Although, I think I was in love long before I consciously realized it. You know when someone makes you feel comfortable, at ease, and you open up and share sacred and personal feelings? That's how he made me feel. I knew he wouldn't take advantage of my honesty and sincerity or belittle my insecurities. I trusted him with me.

When he was little, Gunther was a healthy, freckle-faced, adorable boy who appeared (from what I've seen in his photographs) to be full of mischief and confidence. He grew up the younger of two brothers in the tiny mountain village of Sachrang in Germany; literally a stone's throw away from his native country of Austria. Like all young Austrian mountain boys, he wore lederhosen and skied every chance possible.

Gunther, left, and friends, Austria, around 1960.

He says he was an astute and witty student in his one-room schoolhouse that serviced eight grades. The kind of student whose teacher was wise to keep the reins loose, but the space around Gunther stimulating and unusual. He never passed up the opportunity to tune and wax his teacher's skis in place of sitting through a boring lesson that he'd already taught himself. But stories of America and airplanes always caught his attention. He didn't have time for girls, other than the occasional irritation when a few brave ones showed up to join the neighborhood soccer game, or that one exceptional girl who loaned him her pencil sharpener. He freely admits that when she moved away, he was sad.

Gunther, around 1959. I love his freckles.

Gunther's dreams and desire to achieve always dominated his daily actions. In his early twenties, with a German engineering degree, but a poor student of English, his mother suggested he go to the United States to learn the language. "Gunther, look, in this Certified Ski Instructors of Germany newsletter is an advertisement for needed ski instructors in America. You should go," his mother said. A German native, Horst Locher, was the ski school director at Bryce Resort in Bayse, Virginia. He was recruiting European ski instructors and had placed the ad.

On a snowy December day in 1972, Gunther packed up a few necessities and boarded a Pan-Am 747 in Munich, Germany. He and two other German ski instructors heading to Bryce arrived to a balmy 75 degrees in Washington, DC. *How are we going to ski here?* the three of them thought. A few days later at Bryce Resort, they awoke to cold, clear skies and the unexpected, unfamiliar, loud noise of snow machines. "The visual was amazing. We had heard about snowmaking but had never seen it before. We were excited. It got us out on the slopes and working. I felt right at home, even though I was four thousand miles away and couldn't speak the language that I was supposed to have learned over six years of schooling in German Gymnasium.

"The customers at Bryce Resort typically were military families and middle-class, white-collar folk from Washington, DC, who were genuine, friendly, generous, and hospitable. They, and the locals, were always helpful and pleasant," Gunther explained.

"Southern ski areas in the 1970s were about real estate, fast money. As a result, Bryce was booming. In three seasons at Bryce I met a lot of people. Arnold Mooma, Bryce Resort's maintenance chief, was a homemade American guy. He knew everything and proved it, every day. Without Arnold, things wouldn't have worked at Bryce: the compressors, ski lifts, snowmaking, plumbing, electrical, everything! His knowledge and performance earned him respect. Arnold epitomized American ingenuity. His initiative and skill were impressive. What he knew he taught himself or learned on the job. In Germany, you need papers (a formal education) for everything: to be a mechanic, an electrician, a hairdresser, an engineer, a lawyer—anything, you need papers. A lot of losers with papers make it in Europe. Arnold didn't have any papers, just knowledge and performance," Gunther said.

In the mid-'70s, Joe Luter III of Smithfield Foods owned Bryce Resort and Blue Knob Ski Area in Pennsylvania. Gunther knew Blue Knob needed a general manager. With his education, youthful spirit, and work ethic, Gunther drove to Smithfield, Virginia, to meet with Joe about running Blue Knob. Joe agreed. And just like that, Gunther was now running Blue Knob Ski Area. Early that season Luter had sold Blue Knob to his former Wake Forest classmate and North Carolina real-estate entrepreneur Dale Stancil. With the purchase of Blue Knob, Dale inherited Gunther. In 1976, Gunther's new boss negotiated a deal with the bankruptcy court to lease the flailing Sugar Mountain Company in North Carolina for one season. Dale transferred Gunther to

Banner Elk, making him a very young but spirited, dedicated, and hard-working general manager.

The leftover establishment and property owners of the defunct Sugar Mountain Company didn't take well to their twenty-three-year old, foreign accented, hands-on, get-dirty-if-the-job-requires-it hired leader. "Who is this grease monkey with dirty hands running this place? He'll never last," rambled one of Sugar Mountain's prominent, wealthy, female investors in the failed Sugar Mountain Company.

That first year, Gunther opened the ski area in mid-November. Unheard of in the Deep South, and reason for additional disdain from the community. Plus he began grooming the slopes. Another unusual strategy, and more reason for snickering. The trailblazer paid no attention and continued to run the ski area his way. Before the other local ski areas even opened their doors, Gunther had $200,000 in the bank. By season's end, skier visits had doubled, and ski-related accidents had dropped 75 percent over the previous season.

Fourteen years later, when I first visited Sugar Mountain, Gunther was still there. And in 2016 he celebrated his fortieth year successfully leading Sugar Mountain Resort, Inc. Not bad for a grease monkey.

As you can imagine, Gunther tried to make me believe he was better at sports than I. He wasn't. I laughed every time he bravely made the effort. Our relationship took a turn one day when, while we were working out together, he kissed me. Holy cow! That was a startling and unexpected experience. But an inevitable one. The stars were aligned. No sense denying destiny. Love was powerful and took over. We became inseparable and still are, admiring each other and growing tighter with time.

We got married in 1997 at St. Mary's Church back in my

hometown. The small and special ceremony included fifty people. Gunther was on crutches, because two weeks prior to our wedding we'd been playing tennis when he fell to the ground after a sudden, sharp pain in his ankle. See, he was still trying to outpace me at sports! Will he ever learn?

He yelled at me, no joke, YELLED at me: "Kim! Why did you throw your racket at me? You hurt my ankle."

"What? My racket is right here in my hand. I didn't throw it at you. Are you crazy?" I ran over to his side of the court to see how I could help.

I have no idea where his conclusion came from. Needless to say, he tore his Achilles tendon all by himself. I did not throw my racket at him.

He hobbled down the aisle and married me. Despite his physical failings, I said "I do" too. To transport us and the wedding party from the church to the reception, I surprised everyone with three old fashioned cars that were lent to me by a few locals who respected and admired Krista's and my dedication and accomplishments as ski racers: a 1920s red-and-black convertible Model T for the two of us, a 1930s green Packard Rumble Seat Coupe for the groomsmen, and a 1950s red convertible American Rambler for the ladies—Krista, Sherri, and my college friend, Roxanne. We danced, ate, and drank the afternoon away. Anyone who knows Gunther won't be surprised to learn that we never took a honeymoon because it was imperative that we get right back to work. Today he justifies that sacrifice with, "Kim, every day is a honeymoon."

I'll go for that.

Life moseyed on. I became more involved in the business of Sugar Mountain and the community, spending ten years on the Village of Sugar Mountain planning board. Listening was my greatest asset in the first several years, since I didn't know much about official municipal meetings or the function of a planning board. The Village of Sugar Mountain is a small community. So when a willing citizen agrees to a community service nomination, the position is often theirs, *forever*. I observed the behavior of the productive chairman and became versed in Robert's Rules of Order. Later, I contributed with conviction. I wasn't always in step with the status quo, but I welcomed the older, more seasoned members allowing my voice to be heard and sometimes even passing a motion I initiated.

Additionally, Sugar's director of operations, its marketing director, and I represented Sugar Mountain Resort at each semi-annual North Carolina Ski Area Association (NCSAA) meeting. The nonprofit organization is the official trade group for North Carolina ski areas. It fosters, stimulates, and promotes snow sports, and snow sports safety in North Carolina. The Organization sells a limited number of gold cards (ski/snowboard passes valid for any North Carolina ski area throughout the winter season) and collects membership dues in order to leverage its goals and function productively. In no time, I was appointed treasurer.

A small, eclectic group of dedicated men founded the North Carolina Ski Areas Association in the late seventies. Grady Moretz, owner of Appalachian Ski Mtn., Rick Coker, owner and operator of Cataloochee Ski Area, and Gunther collectively and passionately cultivated an anomaly: North Carolina skiing! Yes, there's skiing, good skiing—NO, excellent skiing in North Carolina. With mountains higher than any east of the Mississippi, North Carolina skiing endures the ebb and flow of winter at 36 degrees latitude and -81 degrees longitude, equivalent to North Africa's global latitudinal position. Average annual snowfall is about eighty inches. If we're lucky and take the risk, ski seasons run from early November until late March. Relentless rain and 50 degrees is a given once or twice throughout a winter season. But so is -5 degrees and 50-mph winds. Two feet of snow comes every now and then. Shutting down the ski area in mid-January because tropical weather bullies the Arctic back up north isn't unheard of. Once the arctic weather has the courage to fight back, the ski areas scurry to life again. Technology, experience, anguish, snow management, patience, stress, persistence, mental despair, people, and sound management get us through the season every time.

Without flinching, whining, or stumbling upon variables beyond its control, this unlikely skiing region of the world produces a faithful product and pumps out new skiers and snow-boarders in the hundreds of thousands every year. It introduces the joy of snow—imagine, SNOW—to its guests, most of whom have never even seen or touched it. All well worth its weight in snow—I mean gold. It's a profitable business . . . most of the time.

Just when life was moving along at a comfortable and pleasant pace, it threw me a curveball. In 1999, I was two months pregnant when I started bleeding. Fearfully I considered that something could be wrong, but reasoned that it was probably normal. *Nothing to worry about.*

I told Gunther. He encouraged me to see the doctor, and I did.

Everything was *not* okay. There was no heartbeat. It was heartbreaking. My doctor scheduled a D&C the next morning, and sent me home.

That evening, we had made dinner plans with some out-of-town colleagues. I just didn't feel up to it, and of course Gunther understood. He reluctantly went without me. Shortly after he left, my body decided to release a child that was never meant to be. The torment was physically and mentally excruciating, worse than anything (knee surgeries, concussions, injuries, tumbles down ski slopes, physical dry-land testing camps,

..YTHING) I had ever experienced. Throbbing, unbearable cramps took over to the point where my head hurt. Streaks of agony reached out like tentacles to the edges of my body. Contractions pulsed routinely with no regard for my God-given level of pain tolerance. For forty-five minutes, I endured nature's effort to protect and cleanse me.

It was out. Relief and exhaustion complemented each other. I stared for what felt like an eternity at strings and strands of unformed flesh, vibrant shades of red and white, disorganized clots of tissue, wondering why my only option was to flush the toilet. Harsh, cruel. That's what it was: harsh and cruel.

I crawled into bed, exhausted, stunned at what had just happened. The physical pain had subsided, and I fell asleep.

The next morning I called my doctor and told him that I had experienced a miscarriage and that there was no need for my scheduled D&C. He told me I should come in any way to ensure everything was okay.

I'm not one to see a doctor if not absolutely necessary because as an athlete I know from experience that my body will heal itself. But I kept the appointment anyway. He examined me. Physically everything was fine. My body worked. Yay.

"Were you able to save anything?" the doctor asked.

Save anything? I thought in a state of shock while melting into myself.

Imagine miscarrying a child . . . ALONE . . . in your own bathroom and having the wherewithal to rummage through potential storage containers, scoop it out of the toilet, keep it overnight, and transport it to the doctor's office like it was no big deal. Like it wasn't a potential child. A dead child.

"Um . . . no. I didn't even think about that," I said, emotionless, hoping I was disguising my state of shock and psychological despair.

"If you had, we could have tested the tissue to see why you miscarried," the doctor explained compassionately.

Thankfully, a year later Olivia was born. The first three months of pregnancy I was queasy every day. I worried a little about another miscarriage, but not too much, because this time things felt different. Gurgling and tumbling occurred in my stomach randomly and frequently. I often was tired. Periodically I was light-headed, and I craved a green apple every day. I despised meat, and other oddities were happening all the time.

But all went well except for the delivery. I was determined to endure a natural childbirth, no drugs, no epidural, no scheduled C-section. After about fifteen hours of labor at home, my water broke—at least, I suspected that's what had happened. But I wasn't quite sure, so I called the hospital. "Uh, Kim. You need to get here right away."

"Okay. I'm on my way," I said calmly.

I phoned Gunther, and before I knew it he had arrived home, scooped me up, and had me in a birthing room twenty minutes later. The ride typically takes thirty minutes. Krista was not far behind. She was my support (Even though I really didn't think I needed any. That's what hospital personnel were for, I secretly thought.) while Gunther paced the hallways. Olivia couldn't get through the birth canal, and after about six more hours of painful effort our vitals were showing dangerous, life-threatening signs of distress. Rapidly I was prepped for surgery, sliced open and Olivia was safely brought into the world in November of 2000.

JOY! At last, peaceful joy.

Gunther was a mess, and Krista was over the moon with excitement and relief.

Gunther and I loved, cherished, and protected our new baby girl like all good parents do. Naturally Olivia was an overachiever—like everyone's kid, right? She mastered walking and talking well before she was a year old. Learned to ski just after her second birthday, and grasped swimming a few months later. She could read books by four, and recite every television or radio commercial from memory word for word . . . the list goes on and on and on!

I see you rolling your eyes. For that I'll torment you some more. Olivia learned to ride her pink bike without training wheels by four years old. She could say her ABCs from start to finish before she was three, and she could do backward and forward flips underwater just before her fourth birthday. I know. I know. I'll quit now.

But there's more!! Okay, okay, enough already. I get it. I'll stop.

Gunther has his strengths at childrearing, and I have mine. Olivia picked up on that right away. One night, shortly after she was put to bed and we were cozied in for the night, Olivia reappeared. "Daddy, you fluffed my pillow but forgot to tuck me in," she said.

He followed her to her room and preciously tucked her in.

Sucker!

Love, marriage, and a baby! It's a wonderful time in the life of a girl.

One morning when I got a chance to sleep in, Olivia made me breakfast. My place at the kitchen table was neatly set. A champagne glass of freshly squeezed orange juice, two strawberries, a wine glass of Sugar Smacks, and a slice of buttered and jellied toast waited for me. My heart melted and I ate every bite, even though I wasn't hungry.

"Madam President, why isn't there a picture of skiing on the North Carolina Department of Transportation's (NCDOT) road map?" Grady Moretz asked.

He'd just called me Madam President! One of Southern skiing's patriarchs, a founder and former president of the NCSAA, a National Ski Area's Associations (NSAA) Lifetime Achievement Award recipient, the Order of the Long Leaf Pine Award recipient, a mover and a shaker in every corner of North Carolina's High Country and beyond, just called *me* Madam President. I was beside myself, bursting with pride and fearing for my integrity in the event I didn't respond like the Madam President should.

Answer the question, Kim. Pull yourself together. Get back on Earth, preferably in the boardroom.

I didn't know the answer.

Say something.

Voices kept echoing in my head; talking over each other.

"Grady, I don't know the answer to your question. But I will certainly find out and begin efforts for a winter picture in the next DOT road map," I calmly and confidently replied.

The room was filled with at least five men and only one other female. My first meeting as the elected North Carolina Ski Areas Association's first female Yankee president went on without a glitch.

In the spring of 2002, six years after serving as treasurer, I had been elected president of the NCSAA for the first time. I had every intention of taking the organization to a higher level, making it better than it already was. I saw the road and executed each project systematically.

Updating, printing and distributing the neglected NCSAA's brochure was my first order of business as the new NCSAA president. It was not an easy one. Submitting data, pictures, and descriptive text to a new, unproven leader took the backseat for most of the ski resorts' key managers and owners. It simply fell off their radar once the meeting adjourned. After all, they had ski areas to operate. I called, emailed, left messages, sent letters, followed up in every way I knew how. The previous brochure designer had had the brochure on his desk for years. I hired a new designer, had the camera-ready brochure available for viewing, a print quote, and a distribution plan on the fall meeting agenda. The project was approved and executed in time for the 2002-2003 winter season. Missing and critical brochure data from members who'd "forgotten" to submit it was provided on the spot.

The second order of business was building a flexible, useful, creative website. www.goskinc.com came alive in 2003. Presenting all North Carolina ski resorts equitably and appealing to the consumer and the press were the motivating factors. Nine pages included—an introductory home page, a downloadable brochure, a page listing each resort's information with links to each resort's own unique webpage, an updatable slope conditions and snow reporting page, a driving directions and visual state locator map page, a skier safety page, a page archiving the economic impact studies, a gold-card page, and a page discussing the value and importance of snowmaking in North Carolina.

During the 2002–2003 season, our economic impact study

needed to be updated. We hired Drs. Steve Millsaps and Peter Grothius from Appalachian State University to conduct the study. Previous survey questions were reviewed, analyzed, and updated. Surveys were distributed to patrons by staff at each North Carolina ski resort throughout the winter season, then turned in to the professors who compiled the data to produce the final report. A press conference was held at Sugar Mountain Resort in late November. The 2002–2003 report can be found online.

A friendly relationship with the North Carolina Department of Transportation (NCDOT) had fallen through the cracks. State highway road signage to all the North Carolina ski areas, snow and ice removal, and traffic flow during holiday and peak periods needed to be addressed. The NCDOT division engineer, along with his district engineer, attended the 2003 fall meeting. We discussed our concerns. They weren't well received. Shortly after the meeting the DOT responded by letter, stating, "The ski area directional signs that were placed as a result of a 1985 study are adequate and no changes are recommended." Obviously we didn't agree. The board suggested I craft and submit a follow-up letter with requests for changes and additions, and address other concerns as well. No response.

The NCSAA board suggested we seek the help of our state politicians. A list of each ski area's elected officials was compiled, and each representative was invited to the spring meeting. Two North Carolina state senators and two state representatives attended the June 2005 meeting. They heard us. Ski area directional highway signs were added to the existing routes and continue to be maintained. Snow and ice removal improved on state roads, and traffic lights at existing bottlenecks were reprogramed during the busy holiday period and peak weekends. Recently I saw additional unsolicited NCDOT ski area directional highway signs posted at strategic locations throughout North Carolina's mountain communities. We were being heard, and my polite but persistent efforts were paying off for the greater good of the North Carolina ski industry and its consumers.

Another issue facing the NCSAA board was unauthorized gold-card sales. A gold card allows the passholder to ski or snowboard at any of the six North Carolina ski areas throughout the winter season. Prior to my leadership, the association had lost control of gold-card sales. Unofficial websites were acting as gold-card sales agents. Selling the one hundred available gold cards was necessary to fully fund the NCSAA. It took a year and a half to communicate to consumers that the NCSAA was the official and only sales outlet. At last during the 2004-2005 season, all one hundred available gold cards were purchased from the NCSAA.

It was time to modernize our tired, dated TV commercial, and it was advantageous to rekindle our relationship with the North Carolina Division of Travel and Tourism (NCDTT). We hired a media production company and organized video shoots at three of the North Carolina resorts. The final product was a fresh, attractive, and enticing new commercial. The board invited the NCDTT and its advertising agency to attend the fall meeting. Collectively, we drew up a marketing plan that included the newly produced TV commercials. A thriving and productive partnership continues today. In 2005, the association began distributing one or two press releases annually to a growing database of local, regional, and industry-wide media personnel.

The North Carolina Skier Safety Act, adopted in 1981, lays out the responsibilities of the skier and the ski area operator. It is a law designed to fairly and equally protect both parties. In 2005, the NCSAA thought it prudent to reexamine the law and tighten up a few ambiguous sections. We hired the Roberts and Stevens law firm from Asheville, North Carolina. The undertaking proved as difficult as expected, even though very little resistance popped up. Nonetheless it was arduous and time-consuming. Passion, knowledge, and complete dedication from a handful of ski area owners/operators and our two-man law team can take credit for the revision. On July 27, 2009, the North Carolina General Assembly updated and revised the North Carolina Skier Safety Act.

I led the NCSAA until 2006, and then it was time for someone else to take over. After all, this was a volunteer job, not one of those six-figure corporate board positions that comes with a built-in administrative assistant and a staff of MBAs! The decision makers nominated a new slate of leaders, which included me as treasurer once again for the next four years.

In 2010, I was back as the association's president. Still am today. At just about every NCSAA fall meeting Grady Moretz continued to hold the NCDOT road map in the air and wonder out loud why North Carolina skiing still wasn't represented. Of course I took note. I continued to submit pictures, make phone calls, and even invited the state's official photographer to do a photo shoot at any convenient North Carolina ski resort. We would provide models, lift/slope tickets, and lunch if necessary. Persistence and kindness eventually paid off. The 2011–2012, 2013–2014, and 2014–2015 DOT maps all contain pictures promoting North Carolina skiing.

Much of the groundwork for revitalizing the NCSAA was laid during my first term as president. My second term has been about staying current in an imaginative and visionary way without eroding the fundamentals of our mission. We persist in updating and distributing the brochure and communicate via press releases. Gold cards sell out, at a record-breaking pace some years. Updated commercials for every medium—web, TV, and other digital platforms—have been produced and distributed through thoughtful and affordable mediums. Our website was modernized. Positive and complementary relationships endure with the NCDOT and NCDTT. During the 2014–2015 season, another economic value analysis study was conducted by RRC Associates, a recognized leader in consumer intelligence and strategic market research for the tourism and recreation industries based in Boulder, Colorado. The value study was followed up with a press conference at Sugar Mountain Resort in mid-November. But most important, competitive entities work together toward a common goal.

My first visit to North Carolina back in 1990 laid the footing and constructed the pillars that became the foundation for my professional career, whether I was serving a board or on the clock. Modernizing the perception of North Carolina skiing was my goal. It still is. I hit the ground running, jumping over, crawling under, or simply walking around any obstacle that popped up. I latched on to anyone who showed signs of support—either for themselves or for the greater good.

Civilian life. It's broader and more spacious than the life as a US Ski Team member. But it still requires every characteristic I discovered while growing up on the team. Working cooperatively with people created wonderful opportunities to accomplish my goals, all of which have given me a sense of freedom and purpose. I sometimes wonder: Where would I be—and more importantly, who would I be—without the experiences I had as a member of the United States Ski Team?

NCSAA 2015 fall meeting, honoring Grady Moretz's contribution to North Carolina skiing. STANDING: Tammy Brown, Chris Bates (both Cataloochee Ski Area), Gil Adams (Beech Mountain Resort), Michael Wagenseil (Cataloochee Ski Area), Rick Bussy (Wolf Ridge Resort), me, Charles Stancell (Wolf Ridge Resort), Gunther, Brad Moretz (Appalachian Ski Mtn.), Jim Cotrell (French Swiss Ski College), Drew Stanley (Appalachian Ski Mtn.), Ryan Costin (Beech Mountain Resort), Erich Schmidinger (Sugar Mountain Resort). SITTING: Brenda Moretz, Grady Moretz, Reba Moretz (all Appalachian Ski Mtn.).

CHAPTER SEVEN
Together

In addition to volunteering for civic and industry positions, I continued to do my job at Sugar Mountain Resort. Sugar's event schedule was near capacity and humming along at a manageable and efficient pace. I began to work with department managers on program development, execution, and follow-up. We analyzed existing programs, infusing lagging programs with new energy or a different approach. Hopeless programs were eliminated. Performing programs and events never fall off the radar; after all, they're the bread and butter—the frontrunners. We monitored those closely, streamlining and tweaking whenever necessary.

In 1998, we opened Sugar's double–black diamond slope, Whoopdedoo. It was staked, cut, and laid with snowmaking pipes over the summer months. It was a fairly easy addition. The following year, the terrain park was designated and the tubing park was established. Snowshoeing was added to the list of winter offerings at the turn of the century, and I officially became Sugar's director of marketing, events, and programs. After nearly ten years of tutelage and mentoring under Gunther's firm, professional, and knowledgeable leadership, my bones began to grasp and feel his passion for perfection. I understood his business philosophy and agreed wholeheartedly.

I was on a mission to promote Sugar Mountain Resort as broadly as I could and to anyone who would listen. My creative abilities woke from hibernation and roamed into newer territory. It was an easy message to deliver, really: Skiing is fun, especially in North Carolina, and everyone should try it.

We use every medium: print, radio, press releases, direct mail, brochures, local partnerships, email, Instagram, and the World Wide Web to promote Sugar, but do so cost effectively. We don't set a marketing budget based on gross revenue or industry standards and then spend. Our strategy is backward, some might say.

I say it's flexible.

Sugar's information technology (IT) manager and graphic designer is a down-to-earth mastermind. We get along well. Like all IT guys, he's a little quirky and awkward, moody for sure, and typically introverted. We're about the same age and have worked for Gunther for nearly the same time period. He's the brainy, dry type: he's all about logarithms, code, formulas, bandwidth, terabytes. He has a dark, sterile office, and wears the same sneakers every day. Most days he comes to work with nothing: no backpack, no lunch, no snacks, NOTHING. If it's frigid out, he'll wear a jacket. Otherwise it's just a T-shirt that says something we're all supposed to read and understand. Like *WYSIWIG*, *Meh*, and *There are 10 types of people in the world: Those who understand binary and those who don't.* (Get it? I bet you don't. If you do, you understand binary. If you don't get it, you're normal.) and, *I'm only wearing black until something darker comes along* and, *No, I won't fix your computer.* You know, that kind of person.

I'm the creative, get-in-front-of-the-camera, talk-talk-talk-about-Sugar type. I bring a backpack to work every day—usually filled with my laptop, sometimes filled with homemade chocolate chip cookies for everyone and hot chocolate fixings (whole milk, raw chocolate, heavy cream). My cookies are award-winning. Not once, but three times they won the blue ribbon at the

Avery County Fair. First in 2007, a second time in 2010, and then again in 2016. However, I'm not always a winner: I entered my raspberry jam as well. It didn't receive anything. No honorable mention, zilch. Being the competitive girl that I am, I didn't take it well.

I wear a different cold-weather hat each day. My office is airy, bright, and decorated with inspiring posters and pictures. Sticky notes clutter my computer screen. I've got a lot of ideas, all of which come with extreme enthusiasm. The IT guy makes them happen technologically, with no fanfare, little emotion; he questions me only when he doesn't like it. But then, BING! There's my idea on paper, digitally, on the web, wherever!

"You got it! That's it, that's exactly what I envisioned or scribbled on paper. You did it! Thanks," I often say, then walk away to deliver the piece.

Oh brother! is probably what he's thinking.

But I continue to bribe him with my homemade chocolate chip cookies or high-end coffee. He provides me with spring water for my coffee machine. I don't even like coffee.

We work together on marketing, analytics, logistics, tracking, and the execution of events and programs.

In 2001, the North Carolina General Assembly authorized various municipalities and counties, including the Village of Sugar Mountain, to levy a three-percent room occupancy tax. I was among five members nominated by the Village Council to serve on the tourism development authority (TDA) board. One-third of the annual revenue is earmarked for village capital improvement, and the remaining two-thirds for marketing and promoting the Village.

For ten years, I endured the political bickering, inferring that the goal to allocate marketing and infrastructure funds for the betterment of the community in the interest of tourism wasn't straightforward. Seldom did all five members agree. Spending other people's money became foolishly liberal. Wasteful. And discussions often turned nasty and downright offensive. The constant push and pull among members was draining.

"I'm quitting," I said to Gunther more than a dozen times.

After eight years as a board member and two years of chairmanship, I stepped down. Despite the anguish, the drama, the disagreements and the epically long, seemingly unproductive meetings, we did accomplish quite a bit.

On the marketing side, we developed a website: www. seesugar.com. Print ads were directed toward attracting out-of-town and out-of-state visitors. We created SugarFest, an event complete with fireworks, lodging discounts, equipment demos, food and drink specials, an ice show including Olympic silver medalist, Paul Wylie, and my preseason ski clinic including Diann Roffe, two-time Olympic medalist. This annual event still symbolizes the unofficial start to the winter season. We developed and distributed a brochure highlighting four playful seasons within the Village of Sugar Mountain. The board made financial contributions to local chambers and approved support for local tourism-related activities. Specific one-time promotions went out via radio, print, and direct mail. Much to my adamant disapproval we even purchased local billboard space. (Why superficially clutter a beautiful mountain community? Billboards mask the very product we sell, embrace, and love. Nature! Members didn't see my point. I was out-voted.)

The Tourism Development Authority organized and funded the free transportation program that continues to serve the hundreds of thousands of winter tourists who descend upon the community every winter. To me, it seems logical that public transportation would fall under "infrastructure expense."

The board argued and argued over that one, but it remains a marketing expense. I was out-voted again.

TDA contributions to the Village infrastructure added to the aesthetic and upgraded the quality of offerings and activities. An informational kiosk was constructed near the Village entrance. A greenway trail was cleared along Sugar Mountain Drive. Tourism and lodging-related wooden-routed signage was erected throughout the Village. The municipal tennis program receives annual TDA funding, as does the public works, to guarantee an attractive and beautiful Village landscape—flowers! Who can vote against buying flowers? The hefty tab for an upgraded irrigation system for the municipal golf course was picked up by the TDA too.

The Village of Sugar Mountain TDA provided the down payment and continues to meet monthly loan requirements for the construction of the Dave Nixon Pro Shop. The Pro Shop serves as the golf and tennis center during the summer, and the tubing and ice skating center in the winter. The parking lot, which services the Pro Shop, was paved with TDA funds.

Clearly we agreed on some things.

The board continues to take on projects that serve the mission well. The TDA paid for an ice control storage shed, and installed street lighting along Sugar Mountain Drive.

Pre-K came just in time. Juggling Olivia while keeping up with my civic and ski association commitments and my growing responsibilities at Sugar Mountain Resort required cerebral gymnastics, the physical endurance of the world's best female marathon runner, and the patience of Job simultaneously. My toddler tested me, refusing to nap when I needed her to, questioning me when I didn't have the answers, and demanding things I couldn't or wouldn't provide. Initiating diverse and fun learning experiences like story time at the public library, discovering every playground or hands-on museum within a twenty-five-mile radius, sledding, building snowmen, ice skating, skiing, hiking the beautiful trails along the Blue Ridge Parkway, making goop (a mixture of flour and water), and baking were just as fun for me as they were for Olivia. I loved almost every minute of life with my adorable and precocious little star.

Somewhere in between I'm pretty sure I continued to be the twinkle in Gunther's eye.

Three hours a day, two days a week, Olivia went to the Boone United Methodist Church's pre-K program. Those three hours were liberating. But only from the demands of my three-year old. No matter where I was, work demanded my attention, and I thrived on the stimulation and invited additional responsibilities.

Sending her off to first grade, however, wasn't liberating for me like pre-K or kindergarten had been. Olivia and I walked hand in hand from my car to the school's main entrance. She was adorably dressed in a long pink skirt, Hello Kitty top, and pink sandals. Her Barbie lunchbox was strung around her arm. Her shoulder-length wavy blond hair was a little messy. We entered the school, rounded the corner, walked past the principal's office, down a long, crowded hallway to the first-grade classroom. I was excited to meander through the room, talk with the kids, fiddle with the chalk, and sit in a miniature wooden desk.

Suddenly, without allowing me so much as a glimpse into the first-grade room, Olivia gave me a quick hug and basically shoved me down the hall, in a gentle and polite way. I wasn't needed anymore. She was excited to see her new classroom. Her friends from kindergarten all rallied together, talking, giggling, having fun. A delightful sight.

Olivia, first day of first grade, 2007.

What about me? Moms want to have first-grade experiences too! I walked away from the classroom, through the hustle and bustle of the hallway, past the crowds of elementary-age kids. I tried with all my might to look straight ahead, not look back. My protective, loving maternal instincts were powerful, uncontrollable. I turned my head at least three times to see if Olivia was really okay. Hoping she'd say or better yet yell, "Mommy, one more hug." But NO. No voice bellowing from behind, needing me. Only the first-grade teacher catching my eye, her facial expression saying, "She'll be okay. You will be too!"

I got into my car and a flood of tears rolled down my cheeks. I sat for a while and just let it happen before heading to work. Even though the demands of motherhood and a career were often overwhelming, they had a way of complementing each other. I would miss my little companion who, during much of the day, would always keep me grounded and active, one way or another.

In 2003, Sugar Mountain Resort and local meteorologist Ray Russell teamed up to provide customized local weather forecasting using on-site weather stations. And the Weather Channel has an online five-day forecast specific to Sugar Mountain Ski Resort. Weather is critical to the ski business. Consumers base their decisions on it, and ski area operators are beholden to its every move. In 2005, Sugar debuted one of the industry's first live-streaming webcams. Today we have four.

Thirteen managers and a handful of assistant managers make up Sugar's executive team. Gunther's got us all working together like a well-oiled machine. He takes his leadership role seriously. He believes to the depth of his soul that leading people effectively and compassionately by example is the key to success. He's firm, disciplined, unwavering, and knows what he's doing, which forces the leery and the weary to abandon ship early on. He listens intently to those who have proven their commitment and knowledge. Then holds them close for advice and support, creating a loyal and useful team. Each manager carries out their responsibilities then lends a hand when a colleague's in need. Individuals of his management team are no fly-by-night characters. Many have been employed at Sugar between twenty and forty years. The former director of operations began working at Sugar the year it opened, 1969. He retired in 2015.

One season I wanted to be a snowmaker, because it's unique work, and a parking attendant, since that's the first employee our customers encounter. I wanted to talk to them, hear what they said, make them happy, or appreciate and experience their excitement when they arrived. I even had the mountain operations manager purchase a snowmaker's suit in my size. Snowmakers and parking attendants spend most of their time outside and the suit keeps us warm and dry. Midway through the season, I wondered where my suit was and why I wasn't on the schedule for either position.

I heard through the grapevine that a new guy about my size was assigned my suit. I still haven't figured out why those positions didn't work out for me. That season I made it a point to drop off cookies to the parking guys on cold, busy days.

A half dozen or so essential, full-time, established Sugar employees don't have a degree, hold a title, or carry a business card. But their responsibilities are heavy and their performances say it all. They're behind the scenes, keeping the columns of the operation strong, delegating and executing from experience. They handle the on-mountain logistics and ensure a quality product.

At the height of the winter season, Sugar employs five hundred people. Another two hundred find employment in food service. About fifteen part-timers tend to the summer offerings, and approximately twenty full-timers hold down the fort throughout the summer and plan for the upcoming winter season.

In 2005 Gunther added Sugar's director of merchandising duties to my list of responsibilities. That meant I was accountable for the performance of two retail locations. I oversaw a manager, staffing, purchases, inventory management, sales, promotions, marketing, and many unglamorous details. It was also an opportunity to recreate the sports shop's character and guarantee that I was always fashionable on the slopes.

I had a goal to increase sales by 25 percent immediately. The first things I did that spring and summer were clean, reorganize, paint, add and change displays, and rework the consumer traffic flow. Next, I worked with a new manager on purchases, inventory management, pricing guidelines, stockroom organization, and reporting procedures. We laid out employee objectives, tasks, expectations, and implemented an employee incentive program. Sales increased by 35 percent that season.

I'm still working on doubling revenue. That takes time, favorable weather, and a down-to-earth, committed, and dedicated manager. I have the latter. The other two are unpredictable but I'd like to think inevitable. In 2009 we came close, increasing sales by 74 percent. That winter produced 136 inches of natural snow, 122 skier days, record skier visits, and one of Sugar Mountain Resort's highest-grossing revenue seasons to date. We took full advantage of the luck and hustled our buns off.

"Kim, did you hear about the new YMCA coming to Avery County?"

"No, Bill, I haven't. I grew up going to a YMCA in Massachusetts, even won my first blue ribbon there competing in a swim meet when I was a little girl," I said.

Bill's the sign guy. Drive through Avery County and most wooden, routed, meticulously crafted signs are Bill's talent on display. Many of our mountain town ordinances require wooden routed signs, because it makes the community look nice and adds to the indigenous beauty. He does a lot of work for Sugar Mountain. I was picking up signs and we got to chattin', as we always do.

"I'm on the board. Would you be interested in serving?" Bill asked.

"Yes, of course. I'd be honored," I said. It was 2006, and I had just stepped down from my first two terms as president of the NCSAA.

These parts weren't familiar with a YMCA. But I was. I knew firsthand the power and impact a Y could have on its community.

Next thing I knew, I was sitting in a boardroom surrounded by business owners, bankers, healthcare professionals, educators, religious leaders, the sign guy, and a few of the politicians of Avery County, listening. A few still carried that thick mountain slang, making my keen attention even more important. My eyes and ears moved to each member as they spoke. I soaked it all up, trying to gain an understanding of the group's tone and overall mission. The conversation among members, the content, the chairman, the executive director, the silence from many members, and the feel in the room taught me how to fit in.

Upgrading the quality of life for the citizens of Avery County and the surrounding mountain community was the singular goal.

In 2003, Tom Cousins, a successful Atlanta land developer who also happened to be a generous, caring philanthropist, wondered what could make life better in the beautiful mountain community where he and his family spent time. He was well connected with John Blackburn, an Avery Country native who meticulously operates the exquisite 122-year-old Eseeola Lodge and Linville Golf Club, and Dr. Phyllis Crain, who over a short twelve years reinvented the one-hundred-year-old Crossnore School, which provides mountains of hope for children in situations of crisis and despair. Phyllis added six new cottages and built a new charter school, Crossnore Academy, from the ground up. She installed a fiber-optic computer network, athletic fields, a fine arts center, and an equestrian complex and raised the school's endowment from $500,000 to more than $21 million. Phyllis's work is an extension of the school's founder, Dr. Mary T. Martin Sloop.

John and Phyllis understood the needs of Avery County.

"John, what's the one thing that would make life better in Avery County?" Tom asked.

"A wellness center at the hospital," John replied.

"Phyllis, what's the one thing that would make life better at the Crossnore School?" Tom asked.

"An indoor pool so my children could learn to swim," she replied.

From there, Tom initiated the crazy idea that a mountain community of seventeen thousand inhabitants should have a YMCA. Normally the YMCA of the USA doesn't charter an independent Y in communities with less than thirty-five thousand people. There's no way this small community can support such a facility, it was thought. Building a Y was a noble idea, but a recipe for failure.

In 2004 Phyllis, John, Tom, and Stuart Dickson formulated plans and put together an exploratory committee for a Y in Avery County. Two years later, an application for YMCA affiliation was submitted. Articles of incorporation quickly followed for the "Linville YMCA." A board was created and an executive director was hired. In October of 2006, the year I was elected a board member, a ground-breaking ceremony took place, and charter membership sales began.

In 2007 charter membership closed with six hundred forty memberships. John's wellness center and an indoor track opened, and I co-chaired a community capital campaign to raise two million dollars. The first annual princess date night, a formal dinner and dance for daughters of all ages and their fathers, grandfathers, or father figures, kicked off while construction began on the Y's Aquatic Center. In 2008 group exercise, locker rooms, massage therapy, and Phyllis's dream of an aquatic center for her Crossnore School children opened.

Between 2009 and 2011, the Y's impact continued. The splash program launched, teaching all Avery County second graders to swim. Another capital campaign began to raise funds for the Hugh Chapman Center, a place for business retreats, festive gatherings and classroom learning. The annual Strong Kids campaign for scholarship and subsidy funds took off. Membership reached three thousand, and a collaboration between the Y and Avery County launched efforts to combat obesity.

"It was an exciting time for Phyllis and me. We had such a great time dreaming about a YMCA in Linville. The process took many twists and turns, but it was truly the best project of my lifetime. Phyllis has to be looking down from heaven with a smile on her face seeing all those Crossnore kids learning to swim," John said.

In July of 2012, after a longstanding, hard-fought battle with cancer, Phyllis passed away at the age of fifty-five. Many heartfelt and wonderful stories were told during her "Celebration of Life" ceremony. Tears streamed down my cheeks and my heart melted and ached as friends and family spoke for close to an hour. Gunther looked around for tissues, but couldn't come up with any.

Phyllis wanted the kids at the Crossnore School to have a dog on campus. The health inspector wouldn't allow it. He argued that it wasn't safe, sanitary, proper, along with plenty of other excuses.

"It is safe. It is sanitary, and more importantly it's a healing tool, a source for love, trust, learning and growth for the children," she argued.

"I'm sorry, Dr. Crain, you can't have a dog on campus at the Crossnore School. It's not allowed," the health inspector argued back.

"We are having a dog on campus. You find a way to make it allowable," she told him.

The Crossnore School now has ten dogs; Chloe, Dunkin, Fernando, Benny, Gracie, Sugar, Gabby, Shiloh, Cookie, and Jake, one for each cottage on campus. All have been rescued from local shelters and are the stars of the Crossnore School Pet Nurturing Program.

That's what Phyllis was like. She made it happen.

The YMCA SPLASH program, designed to teach children to swim, was funded by an anonymous donor, and now includes

Pre-k, second grade, and home-school students; roughly 1,500 Avery County children have learned to swim. The Y's Endowment Fund received its first gift. The center offered its first recreational sport, gymnastics, and summer Pre-K camp. The YMCA delivered the Darkness to Light program to help fight against and prevent child sexual abuse. Then came a dance program, snow camp for K-6 students, and a martial arts program. These programs have served over four hundred Avery County children.

In 2013 Tom's crazy and potentially unsustainable idea realized its first year of operation without a financial shortfall. A genuine sigh of relief was felt throughout the board. Sustaining an unsustainable endeavor takes an unending amount of energy, effort, dedication, persistence, discipline, and money.

The YMCA inherited a community nonprofit organization in 2014 that serves individuals at the end of life; this initiated the Y's community outreach and independent living program. The Y took over the county recreational soccer program, increasing participation from seventy-seven to 181. The endowment program reached $100,000, and the Y was deservedly voted Avery County's Business of the Year.

The audacity continues. A campaign for an indoor athletic complex has just begun, and even I was shaking my head; as I mentioned, according to YUSA guidelines, a Y in Avery County was unsustainable. But we keep believing and pushing forward. The powerful preschoolers' program just started and is sure to produce results in the years to come. For the first time since its inception, the Williams YMCA of Avery County is operating in the black, but not from membership dues and program revenue alone. Financing and charitable contributions from generous Y believers just down the street or hundreds of miles away pick up the slack.

It's enlightening to sit at a table with accomplished leaders and compassionate people from industries not my own. To realize and learn that their knowledge speaks from experience, from doing. It's real. It's tangible. It's genuine, and it's making life in Avery County better.

Just like the Y, Gunther and I believe in making a difference. Growing and streamlining are paramount and ensure a stable economy. In 2006 and 2007, Sugar hosted NORBA National Championship events. It took a small, dedicated team one year to organize, and two hundred staff and volunteers to work the competition weekend. Twelve hundred competitors came from eight countries and forty-three states and territories.

Even Olivia competed.

Spectators lined the competition routes and the start/finish area. An impressive amount of money was generated, and the event increased local tourism tax dollars for the month by 66 percent. And importantly, Sugar Mountain, tucked away in the Appalachian Mountains, gained national and international recognition within the mountain-biking community.

In 2007, we built a ten-thousand-square-foot outdoor ice rink. In 2008, Sugar inked 140 consecutive skier days, a record.

Many times Gunther and I have stood on the top of Sugar Mountain, and once Gunther looked into the distance, surveying the five-hundred-acre mountain and said, "We're gonna own this someday, Kim." I believed him.

In 2010, Gunther purchased Sugar Mountain Resort, Inc. from his trusted business partner and loyal friend of thirty-four years, Dale Stancil. A year later, Gunther purchased the Sugar Mountain Trust, which owned the land and everything fixed to it. Many times since purchasing Sugar Mountain Resort, Gunther has ridden the chairlift or driven the snow-cat (a large, tracked vehicle that beautifully grooms the slopes) alone, crying. Tears of pride, accomplishment, and disbelief rolled down his cheeks. He still fills up with emotion, but tries to hold it back when I'm around.

I get it. Men cry too.

For a guy full of energy, motivated by accomplishment, always attempting the impossible, and a John Wayne fan like Gunther, achieving the American dream was inevitable. A boy from a tiny, picturesque, European mountain village, who's profoundly changed an American community and effectively influenced an industry, now owns a mountain in the Southern Appalachians.

Seldom do Gunther and I go out to dinner by ourselves; typically Olivia comes along. When we do, though, we have engaging and stimulating conversations. We listen to each other. But one evening, I didn't want to listen.

My eyes engaged his pretty blues. "Gunther, I have a question: Am I still the twinkle in your eye?"

"No," he said. "You're the sparkle."

2011

CHAPTER EIGHT
Growing

On the outside, Gunther never wavers with his decisions or his commitment. From early November until late March, seven days a week from five a.m. until five thirty p.m. (sometimes longer), he's physically at Sugar, working inside and outside, managing, and most often doing. In mid-January, I get tired. He does too, but his routine is religious.

"Can't you sleep in, just once, not go to work?" I ask.

"No. Things need to get done," he replies.

"Okay," I say. Other times, I'm not so understanding.

As robotic as his routine is, he makes my job easy. The boasting, the message, every word I say publicly when I promote Sugar is genuine.

Living and breathing snow is unusual, and the worry is complex, seldom understood, and rarely communicated. The job is managed professionally, but anyone who has a heart knows that ultimately it's personal. During sleepless nights, sometimes our thoughts are consumed with unyielding, unsympathetic rain and warm temperatures. Manmade snow is worth $2,000 per hour. Thirteen hundred hours is a season average. Yet without concern, the rain beats down and beats down. There's nothing to do but worry and wait. The morning comes. Our eyes are heavy, circles are visible, energy is low, tempers are short, mental strength is weak. But leadership is more important than ever. The next several days or weeks, business may be severely diminished or lost, triggering tough choices involving staffing, payroll, snowmaking, daily slope and lift operations, communications, revenue sources, expenses, short- and long-term plans, and people's lives and livelihoods—whole families', even. But in some cases we are lucky, unaffected. Southern skiers are resilient, grateful to have any passable surface to slide over.

Sometimes this worrisome weather precedes or occurs during a Martin Luther King weekend, a President's Day weekend, or the holiday period. And then we're not solely thinking about the wasted expense, but the lost revenues. One third of a season's income can be realized during those three time periods. Gulp!

It's not shareholders, a board, or a group of investors that do the worrying. It's two people. And a community that takes the hit.

As important as the product is, so is the customer. We listen intently to them, whatever they say and no matter how they say it. Some feedback is hard to digest. But it reminds and pushes us to address problematic and challenging areas. Sometimes customers' behavior gets out of hand and we have to throw them out, or even call the police. That happens because when hundreds of thousands pass through our doors in a short five months, there are bound to be a few who steal, cheat, and lie. The rest of the 99.9 percent simply enjoy their experience.

Approval and praise come in all forms, at likely and unlikely times. "Excuse me, ma'am. My name is Kim. I work here. The *Charlotte Observer* would like me to submit a picture for a ski story they will run in tomorrow's newspaper. Can I take a picture of your boys for the paper?" I asked.

"Oh, yes, please do," the woman replied.

It's frigid outside, a crisp, blue-sky day. The snow crunches loudly underfoot. One streak of exposed facial skin succumbs to frostbite the minute it hits the prickly, stinging air. Sometimes it tickles, but it always turns my cheeks a rosy, healthy red. Though I never get used to the thawing of my frozen, numb toes and fingertips, everything else about being on the mountain is rejuvenating. The snow blowers are running full force and the woman's boys are bundled up tight; facemasks and goggles shield every inch of their faces. Yellow-and-red jester helmet covers playfully protect their heads.

"Where are you from?" I asked.

"Orlando," she said.

"Lots of folks from Florida come to Sugar," I said.

"We come every year. We love it. Sugar is like our Disney World!" she said.

"Disney World!" I exclaimed. "Oh my God, really? What an incredible compliment. For real, this is your Disney World?"

"Yeah!" she replied again, with the same level of excitement she'd expressed the first time.

Wonderment engulfed me. *Disney World! Wow, Disney World.*

The next day, Saturday, January 17, 2009, her boys were on the cover of the *Charlotte Observer*'s Local & State section.

And if that's not reward enough, sometimes when Gunther, Olivia, and I are out to dinner, we notice a family with Sugar Mountain lift tickets hanging from their jackets, talking about their day, sharing selfies or other photographs from the slopes—having a good time. We proudly observe from a distance.

"Gunther, do you have a stash of complimentary tickets in your wallet?" I'll ask.

"Yup, I have five. Should I give them the vouchers?" he questions.

"Definitely."

"Oh, Dad, please don't be a stalker or behave all stealthy," Olivia chimes in. She gets embarrassed.

Believe it or not, being nice is sometimes awkward. We do it anyway.

To keep us organically in touch, Gunther and I go out skiing almost daily, sometimes together and sometimes separately. We ride the chairlift with strangers, engaging in inquisitive conversation. Firsthand information is priceless, informative. Our fingers are on the pulse. It's our stethoscope. How guests receive what the entire crew aims to do every day is just a few feet from the protective four walls of our offices. It's fun, easy, cheap, healthy, and more than a spreadsheet or a survey could ever tell us.

I've long since gotten over my post-competition dislike for skiing, and I love to do it now. I even took up snowboarding several years back. I'll never lose that competitive spirit or the desire to be out in nature. Heck, I go on 25-mile bike rides with guys in their sixties, and have to prove to myself that I can outride them. I'm pathetic. I compete in the Monday night adult ski race league, and get upset when a few twenty-year-old guys beat me. I still feel in my soul that I ski like a World Cup racer. Ski runs are energizing, confidence builders, exciting even to a middle-aged kinda-but-not-really-has-been—or never-was.

I'm still particular about the quality of my equipment and how it performs. My skis have to be tuned properly, and to my preferences. The length and the stiffness of the ski, the angle and sharpness of the edges throughout the length of the ski, and the wax ironed into the base all matter. If any variable is incorrect, I can tell from the minute I step into the binding. Just the other day, my skis kept arguing with me, and wouldn't turn with ease the way I'm accustomed to. It reminded me of an experience in the late eighties when I was racing a Nor-Am giant slalom in Mont Sainte-Anne in the dead of winter.

December days in Canada are dark, cold—even mean. I always felt Old Man Winter was laughing at me while I tried to outsmart him with my attitude. Loaded with energy just to get to the finish line and out of the cold, I popped from the starting gate like a firecracker. I made it to the first gate. That's it. My skis WOULD NOT turn. I wanted to go left, but they went straight. I tried to shuffle them around to make the second gate. Couldn't do it. I could not muscle or finesse my skis to obey my command. I skied out of the course, beelined it down the race hill, past every gate and to the ski lift. Disgusted, I rode the chairlift to the start, picked up my training skis, and took the gondola back to the base of the ski resort. By ten thirty a.m., my day was over. But not before finding revenge. Still a teenager, I stomped to the underground parking garage, which was the race circuit's ski-tuning quarters. My equipment rep was tuning skis. Next to his workbench was a sturdy, industrial-size trash can. I threw my skis into the trash can. He was scared. Asked if everything was okay. It wasn't. *I work hard, suffer through injuries, and for my equipment to end my day is unacceptable,* I thought.

I've grown up since then, and as a result have encountered some tough stuff that just seems to have come along uninvited. Not often, but once is more than enough. A faint and repetitive noise comes from the northwest. The whooping sound begins to hasten and magnify. I get a lump in my throat. My stomach feels sick. I freeze and hope it isn't what I think. Curiosity and a sense of responsibility sparks me from the comfort of a peaceful winter evening and a dark night. I hurry to the window and in the distance see one blinking red and two still green lights making their way hastily up the valley, maneuvering closely around and in between terrain that reaches well into 6,000 feet. The whooping sound is loud, easily identifiable now. It's Wings Air Rescue. They provide aeromedical transportation for critically ill and/or injured patients. The night rescue route into Banner Elk takes them directly over our house. *Whoosh!* With speed and purpose the helicopter passes overhead.

The obtrusive sound awakens everything in its path, and I wonder and worry who is hurt while simultaneously considering the courage, determination and selflessness of the guys and gals who pick up the pieces of tragedy. Is it a late-night car wreck or are they headed to Sugar Mountain to pick up one of our night-skiing session guests? No matter the reason, it creates a sinking and helpless feeling in me. Rarely, the phone rings and Gunther is notified of a situation that creates a slew of behaviors and emotions in him. But most of the time the night moves on, the morning comes, and I wonder who took that ride to the Johnson City Medical Center and are they okay?

More than any ski area would like to admit or face, it gets sued. That's just what the world is like today. Sugar is a small business. We hire a regional, competent law firm when necessary. We don't have an in-house legal department.

Gunther knows more about the operation of our ski area than the plaintiff attorney, the defense attorney, the plaintiff, the expert witnesses, the jury, and the judge combined. He defends the actions of Sugar Mountain Resort daily and when necessary in a court of law unquestionably and professionally. He knows what's beneath every unturned stone, the consequences of every action; he can spot the holes in the story of a fast talker and a liar only because he has experienced all of it once or a thousand times.

How could he not contain abnormal amounts of knowledge and information when for forty years he's been on the job twelve hours a day, 120 days straight? He only reverts to an almost-sane man's working schedule throughout the summer months.

The lawsuits and accusations weigh heavy, especially ones that expect a $19,000,000 reward, go to a jury, and are no fault of the ski area. Lesser suits take their toll as well.

Sure, the numbers at the end of the year tell the story, but when the parking lots are overflowing weekend after weekend, and generation after generation visits Sugar, we know the strategy and the system are working. The fun, the passion, the work, the reward, the challenge, the opportunity for growth and improvement, and the excitement of a new season is always the energy that drives the present and the future.

Sugar Mountain Resort has been treated well since 1976, and as a result has grown with the times, the demands of customers, and the constant evolution of technology, all with the personal touch of its leadership. In 2014, the Big Red Slope, a wide-open, gentle trail located on the east side of the mountain, was renamed Oma's Meadow after Gunther's mother, Marianne Jochl. *Oma* is a term of endearment and means grandmother in German-speaking countries.

Gunther and his mother on the Chiemsee's Fraueninsel in Germany, 2009.

Photo by Ken Ketchie

Sugar's game-changing slope, Gunther's Way, opened in 2014. I named it. Gunther was reluctant. After all, you name things after dead people. Following several days of conflicting deliberation, Gunther gave in. "You only debate with Kim for so long. Then she wins," he told a reporter.

The Gunther's Way slope wasn't a simple addition like Whoopdedoo. The million-dollar project took many detours and drained Gunther to the point where he threatened to abandon it more than once.

I knew better than to believe he would do anything but continue. His patience and the goal to succeed got the best of him. The nine-acre, 150-foot-wide, 2,900-foot-long, 700-foot vertical-drop slope, its ten new SMI snow-making machines, and the 1,000-gallon-per-minute vertical water pump are just three of the links in a grander development plan for the mountain.

I'm now Sugar's vice president. That means more work, more responsibility, more worry, more stress, and greater authority to share Sugar Mountain. I love that.

Programs that make winter fun affordable give me the opportunity to touch even more people. All Banner Elk fourth graders are learning to ski and snowboard. For years, the Valle Crucis Elementary and Middle Schools have been raising funds through winter fun at Sugar. Pre-K children and their parents are experiencing ice skating through a co-op program with Avery County Schools. Avery County Middle and High Schools support a ski and snowboard club. Home-school and field trip programs reach kids off the mountain. Banner Elk's children are eligible for after-school ice skating discounts. Sugar's enduring ski club not only teaches kids to ski and compete, but gives them the opportunity to experience self-confidence, independence, maturity, and the wonderful virtue of courage.

We're fortunate to be in the business of outdoor winter fun.

Gunther's Way slope under construction (far right).

Ten new SMI snow-making machines.

CHAPTER NINE
Everything Important and Everything Unimportant

Speaking of fortunate, Gunther has been a pilot for over thirty years and loves it. Really loves it. It's his relief, his joy, his passion. The challenge and the freedom of flying fills a space in his soul that nothing else can. We have an airplane, a Piper Cheyenne II. It's a twin-engine turbo-prop; it seats eight, cruises at 260 knots, has a range of about 1,200 nautical miles, and even has a toilet. It's a wonderful luxury, the airplane (and that toilet!). Gunther flew the Cheyenne from Banner Elk, North Carolina, to Straubing, Germany, in 1989 with his best friend, Dick, a retired two-star general in the Marine Corps. Not only does Gunther hold a commercial, multi-engine, instrument flight rules (IFR) rating pilot's license, but he's also a certified Federal Aviation Administration airframe and power plant mechanic (FAA A&P).

He's a German-educated mechanical engineer, so for him, *working* on airplanes is also a stress reliever, a joy, and a passion. Much of his leisure and therapy time is spent with the Cheyenne. We've flown to many, many places in the past, and naturally he intends to fly forever.

Clearly flying is to be part of our life. Forever!

But guess what? Flying in our Piper Cheyenne became problematic for me. Well, more than problematic. It scared me to death. I was afraid, deathly afraid. No joke, I thought I was going to have a heart attack when I flew in the Cheyenne. I did everything to slow my heartbeat to a manageable rate. My hands shook. I broke out in a sweat; my muscles became lethargic and weak. Sometimes I thought my only relief would be to pass out.

Gunther was always very understanding and generously sympathetic of my fears when we flew. He'd often suggest that I sit "right seat" (that's the copilot's position) so I could understand what was going on, or if I was in the back he'd keep me posted throughout the flight. It helped a little but I was still petrified.

I yearned for a solution, and wouldn't you know it—the impossible appeared. This sounds crazy, but one random day in early May of 2013 I looked into the sky and saw a small airplane serenely crossing the horizon. *I can do that,* I said to myself. *I can fly an airplane.* Right then and there I decided I was going to learn how to fly, and I set out to earn my private pilot's license. It was divine intervention, truly, because I would never have made this decision on my own.

The small airport in Elizabethton, Tennessee, forty-five minutes from my home, has a great teaching reputation among the local flying community. I called the Elizabethton Municipal Airport and asked about the flight-training program. I spoke with Dan, the airport manager, who offered a brief background about the flight instructors.

Within a few hours, John, who became my flight instructor, called me on my cell. I was at work. *So quickly?* I thought. I was overtaken with panic. *This isn't real.*

We scheduled an introductory flight for Saturday, May 18, my forty-third birthday.

I arrived on time, and John was there waiting. As we shook hands I was struck by his calm and comforting demeanor. I thought, *This guy's waaay too calm for me. I'll never be able to slow down to his pace.* We walked to the ground instruction room, sat down at the worktable, and talked briefly. He told me a little bit about his credentials. I have no idea what I told him, except that I was afraid to fly.

Okaaaay, I wonder how long this will last? John must have thought.

"Let's go take a look at the airplane," he said, seeming to ignore my fears, while making my desire to fly the priority.

"Okay," I said with scared excitement. John walked slowly, methodically to the spotless, sterile hanger that housed three adorable airplanes. I walked timidly next to him.

There it is: a death trap, I thought.

It was a blue-and-black-on-white Cessna Skyhawk 172, single-engine.

"Go on in," he said.

"In the pilot's seat?" I questioned.

"Yes," he said easily.

That first day, though, it was raining, so we couldn't fly; this was the only reason I could disguise my extreme emotions. I just followed directions, quiet as could be, definitely beside myself. I sat in the pilot's seat. John got in the copilot's seat. I was in awe of the enormous and incomprehensible task that lay ahead and thought, *We are both crazy to even consider me flying this machine!* But I was also excited. I looked at the instrument panel, fixing my eyes on each instrument, one by one. I didn't have any clue what I was looking at. Well, that's not entirely true; I knew some basics from flying in the Cheyenne. But knowing about something didn't mean I could properly apply the knowledge.

Three days later, I was in the left seat of the Skyhawk. John was in the right seat and doing *all* the flying. I did have my hands and feet on the flight controls, but I didn't dare apply any pressure or make any moves short of breathing, in fear of inadvertently causing the airplane to suddenly plummet from the sky.

It was a bumpy day, and John didn't explain that there was no need to worry—and boy, was I worried. With every bump I held my breath and even let out a few *oh no*s. Okay, *every* bump I said out loud, "Oh no!" John was probably thinking, *Either this'll be a short summer for her, or a long summer for me.* I got through the flight—more frightened than I had been before it. *One hour down, thirty-nine more to go.* For some reason, I had it in my head that after forty hours of flight training, I would be home free and I'd have my license. Little did I know that earning a private pilot's license requires a minimum forty hours of flying experience, twenty hours with a flight instructor, ten hours of solo flying, a medical exam, a written exam, an oral exam, and a practical exam—the latter two with an FAA examiner.

After my introductory flight lesson, I bought $320 worth of textbooks, an E6B (a basic, non-computerized aviation calculator that computes true airspeed, heading, wind correction angle, true temperature, nautical miles to statute miles, and so much more), and a plotter, which marks the course of the flight and measures distance on sectional charts. These are stone-age tools, but still useful. It seemed I was committed, financially anyway.

We scheduled another flight for May 23. In the meantime, I was reading my two-inch thick Jeppesen *Guided Flight Discovery Private Pilot* textbook. It was stimulating reading. (I'm serious!) I found the content interesting, and eventually it became addicting. I loved reading it and completed every question at the end of every chapter. Gunther helped me quite a bit when I had questions, or couldn't quite grasp a concept.

Flying became the main topic at our dinner table, and any other time too. Olivia, our twelve-year-old daughter, was not interested. She often had to fight to get a word in during dinner conversations. Eventually her iPhone and iPad occupied her, rather than her parents' conversations.

Throughout the next three months (with the exception of a

three-week vacation in June) I flew at least twice a week, some-times three, learning the basics of flying. It took a solid two months for the voice in my head to stop telling me to quit this craziness. That nasty voice, disguised to think it was protecting me, kept saying, *Kim, you are going to kill yourself and John.* Relentlessly I kept hearing, *Kim, just don't go. Cancel the whole idea. What are you thinking? You don't need to learn how to fly. You can do lots of other things. This isn't important.*

In time, procedures become routine and automatic. I started saying with an unconvincing confidence, "Don't worry, John, I'll get us there," particularly when the approach to land was all wrong. I would be too high or too low, give too much power, not enough power, have airspeed too slow or too fast on final. My execution of the controls was seldom coordinated—a critical skill for a pilot. Every adjustment created some sort of result that I didn't have the experience to anticipate. But I always got us on the ground safely, even if we bounced two or three times down the runway.

Other times I'd come in for a landing with the airplane sideways. One wheel would touch down. Then the other wheel, forced by gravity, physics—whatever natural phenomenon exists—would touch down screeching and pivoting us safely along the runway. Finally the nose wheel would bang onto the pavement. Secretly a wave of relief would ripple through me as I swallowed the lump of tension that had been building up. Unintentionally but aggressively, I would hit the brakes to slow the roll out. Both John and I would take the bouts of whiplash in stride. Not often but every once in a while, I would perform that sideways landing with the grace and finesse only a lucky beginner could pull off.

I even managed to get us in situations that resulted in a go-around because I missed the runway. No, no, no, I didn't land on houses or on the street or crash the airplane. I learned how to go-around and try it again. In the end a go-around became no big deal; it was just part of knowing how to fly in lots of unplanned situations and behaving calmly while executing procedures properly. But believe me, at first I was crumbling inside: my heart racing, blood circulating throughout my entire body at an exponential rate, and genuinely terrified. Surprisingly, my brain did function intelligently and with focused command. How did that happen?

There were still several weeks when I became solidly profi-cient at doing everything wrong. It was reassuring and felt good in an odd and deranged way to know that I could still be alive (and keep John alive too) while performing so deficiently.

John, easygoing and a natural encourager, always calm, never uptight or emotional, said way back in May, "Kim, becoming a pilot is very special. You gain a lot of confidence. Very few people become pilots."

I thought, *Hmm, usually I'm a pretty confident girl. What if this crazy flying experience only makes me a less confident girl, when I fail to earn a private pilot's license?*

Before I was allowed to solo, I had to complete a pre-solo written exam and pass a medical exam. The pre-solo exam was thir-ty-eight questions, a take-home test. It wasn't easy, and it was time-consuming. It took me an entire Sunday (which, by the way, was a gorgeous day) to complete! I found most of the answers in either my two-inch-thick Jeppesen textbook, or that twenty-five-pound 2013 *FAR/AIM* (Federal Aviation Regulations/Aero-nautical Information Manual) book. During the next scheduled flight-training day, John and I looked over my completed exam and made corrections. It was all good, for the most part. I was inching closer to "solo day." What a scary thought that was.

For the next month we practiced the basics, particularly pattern work, over and over again. A pattern is a rectangular route that lays out certain procedures at the specific four points and intersections (crosswind, downwind, base, and final) when approaching an airport to land. Initially, learning the pattern was done on the ground. John drew out a few key mountains and a small lake and the two runways, six and two four, at Elizabethton. (Two four means the runway lies on the earth at 240 degrees (drop the last zero) almost due west, but more accurately west southwest. Three six is due north, or 360 degrees. Get it? Each end of every runway has numbers in increments of ten identifying the direction in which the runway is heading. A pilot knows she is landing or taking off on the correct runway if the heading or compass matches the runway numbers.)

He also listed the airport altitude of 1,800 feet and added 1,000 feet to signify the flight altitude while in the pattern. As he spoke, I made notes on the diagram to help remember what to do and when. I memorized the pattern and all its particulars; I even ran it millions of times in my head during sleepless nights.

The second requirement prior to soloing is obtaining a flight physical from a certified FAA medical doctor. Officially it's called a Department of Transportation Federal Aviation Administration third-class medical and student pilot certificate. I scheduled my appointment with Dr. Davant, a second-generation family doctor practicing in Blowing Rock, North Carolina. I had never seen him before. Gunther sees him, and saw his father before him for his flight physical.

I arrived at the Blowing Rock hospital a little nervous, not about passing the physical but because I'd be another step closer to *having* to solo.

During the exam, Dr. Davant explained that the physical is fairly superficial. The FAA wants to make sure that a pilot doesn't have any illness or condition that could suddenly impair his/her ability to fly. After my physical, Dr. Davant filled out the required FAA paperwork, and in no time I was holding my ticket to soloing.

I was excited, but apprehensive . . . and on the schedule to fly with John the very next day at nine a.m. If all went well, I COULD be soloing tomorrow.

Unable to sleep, I ran the Elizabethton airport pattern in my head over and over and over again, forward and backward: runway six then runway two four. From four a.m. to six a.m. I considered winds, sun, birds, etc., etc., etc. I thought of everything important and everything unimportant. *There's no reason John wouldn't let me solo today,* I thought. In my mind I was ready. I knew I could do it. Thankfully I caught an hour's sleep between six and seven. I arrived at the airport just before nine a.m., pre-flighted (this involves running through a checklist of mechanical and practical items), and off we went.

A flight instructor never tells you in advance when you're going to solo. Supposedly when they are confident with your abilities and your mental and psychological competence, they'll ask you to pull over, tell you you're ready to solo, and step out of the airplane. That day was like every other, not much chatter between John and me—we just got down to the business of flying. It was a cloudy day, and the winds dictated runway six. I preferred runway two four, but I'd have to make six work if I did get to solo that day. There's a weird bit of unstable air above the tiny lake when flying over short final to runway six, which made me slightly insecure.

When we were on pattern number six—no, number seven— actually, I think we were on our eighth pattern (it seems I lost count), I was thinking, *Is this guy going to let me solo or what?* I was getting tired, and the clouds were sinking. *OKAY, we are now on pattern number ten, for sure!* I was starting to perfect my mistakes, and my landings were getting worse with every additional pattern we flew. *He'd better get out soon!* I even looked at John a few times, my eyes radiating the words, *You can get out now. I can do this.* I was going crazy inside.

Finally, after what must have been twelve takeoffs and landings on runway six (John will surely disagree with the number of patterns we did that day. But that doesn't matter! This is my story.), the clouds were sinking. We were holding short for our thirteenth pattern and I was about to transmit over the radio "Elizabethton traffic, Skyhawk 734 Echo Quebec"—that's the identifier, or tail number, of my airplane; *echo* is for *E* and *Quebec* represents *Q*—"departing runway six *again,* Elizabethton," John said he was getting out.

Thank goodness! It's about time, I thought.

He said with calm assurance that instilled confidence and security in me, "Kim, you're ready to solo. Do three patterns, then come back to the terminal."

WHAT? Three patterns? That wasn't part of my plan. *No one ever told me I would have to solo THREE times ALL BY MYSELF. I was prepared to solo ONCE!* a voice in my head snapped.

I quickly got over the change of plans and focused on the task at hand. I was anxious but not scared. I hadn't realized how comforting John's presence was until he got out and I was ALL ALONE. The feeling of emptiness in the airplane was eerie and lonely; John's six foot two and 225 pounds, so he took up quite a bit of space in my tiny Skyhawk. (Okay, it was not MY Skyhawk. It belonged to the airport. But when I flew it, it was *my* Skyhawk.) But no worries, I just pretended he was there the whole time.

Every minute, I talked out loud to myself: "Flaps up, carb heat in, mixture rich, ready for takeoff. Full power, rotate at 55 knots, rudder. Holy cow, this thing took off quick; it just popped into the sky and off the runway. What's up with that? Something's wrong!" Later, I found out that 225 pounds less weight in an airplane that small makes a real difference in its handling. Despite the quick takeoff, everything appeared to be okay. Back to flying: *Climb at 73 knots. Communicate.* "Elizabethton traffic, Skyhawk 734 Echo Quebec's turning right crosswind, Elizabethton."

Look outside, check for traffic. Climb to pattern altitude 2,800 feet and maintain 80 knots. Communicate. "Elizabethton traffic, Skyhawk 734 Echo Quebec's turning right downwind, runway six Elizabethton."

"Moving along—patience. Keep an eye outside, scan instruments. Reduce power to 2,100 rpms, 70 knots, 10 degrees of flaps. Pre-landing checklist: fuel's good, trim set, cabin is secure, mixture's rich, carb heat is out, flaps as required." I was still talking out loud. I envisioned John right next to me. *Altitude with throttle, airspeed with pitch. Descending to 2,400 feet. Communicate.* "Elizabethton traffic, Skyhawk 734 Echo Quebec's turning right base runway six, Elizabethton."

Twenty degrees of flaps, descending to 2,200 feet, reduce power. Communicate. "Elizabethton traffic, Skyhawk 734 Echo Quebec's on final, Elizabethton." *Thirty degrees of flaps, 1,700 rpms, slow this thing down. Approach at 65–70 knots, over the threshold, flare just beyond the numbers, land at 60–65 knots. Keep the airplane straight, a little rudder, ailerons, touchdown, nice and easy, Greaser! Yes, I did it, great landing. Gentle run out.* I let out a huge sigh of relief. I'd landed. I started to breathe again. *Communicate.* "Elizabethton traffic, Skyhawk 734 Echo Quebec's clear of runway six, Elizabethton."

Two more patterns to go.

I got through the next pattern seamlessly. On the second landing, I bounced once, but got the airplane down. There was a lot of tension, anxiety, and stress, but I had done it so many times that truly it was automatic.

I was lined up on runway six and ready for the third and final pattern in order to complete my solo requirement. I transmitted over the radio, "Elizabethton traffic, Skyhawk 734 Echo Quebec's departing runway six, Elizabethton."

I took inventory, assessed the instruments, and took a look outside, ready for takeoff.

"Wait a minute! I can't see the mountaintops. John said THREE patterns! But I can't see the mountaintops. Kim, you're the pilot in command. John said THREE patterns! But I can't see the mountaintops." I was arguing out loud with myself. "I can't fly. I'm required to stay clear of clouds. If I take off I'm going to get in those clouds. I'll panic and crash Dan's airplane. He'll be very upset with me, but I'll be dead."

What do I do? I'll call Unicom.

Timidly, I got on the radio. "John, this is Kim, I can't see the mountaintops. What do I do?" I waited for a response. And waited. And waited. NO RESPONSE. He was not answering me. *No one's answering me! What do I do?* I was nervous. Really nervous. John said THREE patterns. I pushed the throttle forward with my right hand, worked the rudder pedals to ensure a straight takeoff, and held the yoke with my left hand in anticipation of liftoff. My eyes moved from the airspeed indicator to outside the airplane and back again. All the while EQ was speeding down the runway, gaining momentum.

A voice said firmly in my brain, *Kim. You can't. See. The mountaintops.* I pulled the power back, and the airplane decelerated.

I was relieved. But I hadn't accomplished the requirements. *Oh well, I'm alive! That's the requirement as far as I'm concerned!*

John came over the radio. "Kim, what's the matter?"

I said nervously but with confidence, "John, I can't see the mountaintops."

"Okay, let's call it a day. You did great," he said.

I enjoyed a second round of relief and taxied back to the terminal.

I soloed! It counts.

The first thing I did when I got inside the terminal was text Gunther: *Did it!*

He immediately called me. He was super excited and so proud.

I texted Krista: *Soloed!*

Who would have thought I would even have made it this far? Not me. I can assure you of that.

I soloed and I still couldn't believe it.

Flying a solo, round-trip flight of about 150 nautical miles with several stops along the way, is the next required phase to earning a private pilot's license. Keep in mind that I had just recently soloed for the first time, and was by no means psychologically ready to fly by myself on a regular basis, never mind undertaking a long solo cross-country flight!

I was attempting my very first *short* cross-country solo flight to the Virginia Highlands Airport. It was about twenty-five nautical miles away, and I figured that it would take me eleven minutes, plus an additional ten minutes to climb and descend each way; therefore, a round-trip of about forty-five minutes. No big deal. I'd traveled to Virginia Highlands lots of times with John.

But that discouraging voice crept into my head again. It said convincingly, just like it did back in May, *Kim, quit this craziness. With no instructor, you are going to kill yourself! Just don't go. Cancel the whole idea. What are you thinking? You soloed. That's enough. Be proud; move on.*

But my encouraging, confident voice calmly answered back, *Kim, go on. You have the fundamentals. You understand the procedures; there's no reason to feel insecure.*

I'd rescheduled this trip three times because of uncooperative weather. I'd practiced the procedures and memorized all the ground landmarks for three days straight. My brain was exhausted. It felt like I'd never so intensely and continuously studied in this serious and diligent way before.

The day arrived and the weather was just right. I went through the routine: a preflight walk around, preflight checklist, run-up, takeoff, headed for Shady Valley, turned left over the mountain ridge, cruised over South Holston Lake, looked for the Virginia Highlands Airport, and called Virginia Highlands traffic about five miles out. I was by no means calm. Apparently over the radio, I appeared calm and self-assured—so I'm told. Once I flew the approach pattern and was set to land runway two four, I took a look outside. There was the runway, directly below me. *Crap, I can't land. I'm way too high and halfway down the runway. Oh my gosh, I have to go around!* I quickly, nervously recalled the go-around procedures. Since I'd managed to get John and me into lots of go-around situations, practice should make perfect—right?

I executed the go-around procedures as I'd routinely done in the past, but without any instructor to guide me or provide security. I went around for a second time. *Fly the approach; crosswind, downwind, base, final.* I took a look outside. *Altitude is good. Oh no! You have got to be kidding me. I am right of the runway and a quarter of it is behind me. Here we go again. Another go-around.* I went around for a third time. I was disgusted and embarrassed that I had to communicate yet another go-around. *No time for emotions. Get it right, Kim.* I went around again. This time I landed safely. I cleared the runway, taxied to a temporary parking location, and began the process of calming myself down.

It took a while.

My right leg was shaking uncontrollably, and my hands were white. My muscles, my veins, my ligaments, my arteries—every part of me that could collapse was lethargic and jellylike. My spirit was in shock. My entire existence was exhausted and relieved. I had just unintentionally executed two go-arounds! Not one but two, by myself, alone, solo.

Never in all my life were the stakes that high or the emotions so physical. Only when I won that gold medal at the Junior Worlds was the reward that profoundly consequential. And that confidence John had been talking about? Well, I felt it.

Once I calmed down, I taxied to runway two four, took off again, and then settled into cruising altitude—grateful to be on my way back to my home airport. My first attempt to land in Elizabethton was a success. Like always, unless I had a crazy experience, after I secured the airplane, I walked to the ground instruction room in the Elizabethton Municipal Airport, logged my time, and found solace in texting Gunther, Krista, or John—oftentimes all three. A Coke from the McDonald's drive-through was the second phase of post-flight therapy.

CHAPTER TEN
Do Good

For everyone else, flying seemed so easy, even enjoyable. To many it's in their blood. Take Fulton, for example. He's an older gentleman, semi-retired, and usually only works on Sundays and Mondays at the Elizabethton Airport. One summer he asked his wife if he could dip into their retirement account so he could buy an old-fashioned, single-seat, open-cockpit airplane. It's a home-built low-wing monoplane made of wood and fabric, incredibly light. It's called a Fly Baby—a modest airplane!

Fulton refers to his Fly Baby as La Petite Oiseau Rouge. It means little lady red bird. French, obviously. Affectionately named after his mom and wife. His little lady holds twelve gallons of fuel. Has a range of 2.5 hours, about 115 miles in optimal weather conditions. It'll cruise at 75–80 mph. Its empty weight is 690 pounds, but with full fuel and luggage it can handle 925 pounds.

He showed it to me one day, and even let me sit in it. You know when Snoopy flies his airplane? That's how I felt when I sat in Fulton's Fly Baby. I imagined the wind blowing through my hair under my strapped leather helmet, bugs pelting my over-sized black goggles, the air aerodynamically hugging my body while my scarf waved behind my shoulders. I firmly, with two hands, held the control stick located between my legs. My feet rested on the rudder pedals and brakes. I scanned the instruments on the miniature panel and pretended to fly Fulton's vintage aircraft.

If only my cross-country solo could be that effortless and carefree.

Never in a million years did I ever think I would solo, never mind solo cross-country. My cross-country plan was to travel from Elizabethton, Tennessee, through the Tri-Cities (Kingsport, Johnson City, and Bristol), Tennessee, controlled airspace (where I have to talk to the traffic controllers and execute their instructions), to Gatlinburg, Tennessee, to Morristown, Tennessee, back through the Tri-Cities controlled airspace, and then back to Elizabethton. I was nervous on that early morning drive to 0A9 from home. I kept trying to distract my mind with music, at the same time reviewing procedures and the route. I called the automated weather observation service at each airport at least three or four times.

It was a beautiful, brisk, fall Saturday morning: 45 degrees, sunny, calm winds. I arrived at the Elizabethton airport just before eight a.m. and pre-flighted. All was good. I was still nervous, but suppressing it well. I had time to spare, so I sat on the couch, watched TV, and waited for John. I think we'd made plans to meet at eight thirty, with plenty of time for me to depart at nine. John arrived, reviewed my navigation logs, and signed my logbook. I think he sensed that I was nervous, but nevertheless, he proceeded as usual—matter-of-fact, but conveying comfort and a calming assurance. All he said to me was, "Do good."

I boarded the airplane, went through the checklists. I was apprehensive, but deep down—way, way, way deep down—confidence existed. I took off at 9:10 a.m. for my first-ever long cross-country solo trip.

Gatlinburg was coming up, my first planned landing. *Where's the airport? What runway do I take?* Adrenaline was slowly creeping into my system. I spotted the airport. My position and orientation to the airport was confusing me, though. The wind was telling me I should land on runway two eight. Traffic was using runway one zero. *What?* I was talking to myself. *Why are they doing that?* My adrenaline rose several notches higher. *Okay, I'll follow traffic.* But I couldn't get all my flying components to converge. Airspeed, altitude, pitch, timing, communication were all over the place. My mind was racing. But the calm, reasonable, life-saving spirit inside me discreetly entered the back door. *Turning base. Speed is low, add power. Runway coming up quick. Way high. Plenty of runway, Kim* (that's John's voice). *Descending, descending, speed's too fast. I'm descending, halfway down the runway already. Too high, not enough runway. And in a hundredth of a second I'm going around. Pitch up, add power. Reverse carb heat.* "Gatlinburg traffic, 4 Echo Quebec, I'm gonna have to try this again," I communicated. My adrenaline was maxed out, but my survival skills kicked in. *I gotta execute procedures. Slowly milk the flaps up, ten degrees. They have to come up slowly, or else I can lose lift and drop out of the sky.* Gulp.

I was safely in the pattern for the second attempt. I went through the pre-landing checklist. Talking out loud: "Carb heat, crap, forgot to add carb heat. Thank goodness for pre-landing checklist." Without the carburetor heat the engine could freeze up. Making me a goner.

My adrenaline was off the charts now, but I was still in control. My heart was pounding outside of my chest. I set up better for landing that time, but it was still awful. *Who cares! I'm on the ground!*

I taxied off runway one zero and proceeded to runway two eight. I still had the wind issue, though. Traffic was landing on runway one zero. But the windsock was telling me to take off from runway two eight. I didn't want a tailwind for takeoff. I departed runway two eight for Morristown, Tennessee. All was good. I switched weather and communication frequencies for Morristown. Wind said runway five. Traffic agreed. *Great!* Relief at last.

There was lots of traffic at the little uncontrolled Morristown airport. I kept listening. The traffic chatter didn't quit. Airplane after airplane kept calling downwind, base, final. All I knew to do was to properly communicate, and let them know of my position and intentions. So that's what I did. Seamlessly I flew 4 Echo Quebec into the pattern and in among the heavy traffic. I was feeling some pressure to get on the ground the first time. Determined, I got it right and landed on the first attempt—but not without a high bounce and a long float.

When I cleared the runway, I looked around. *What in the world is going on? Airplanes everywhere: old ones, single-engine airplanes, a jet, biplane, war airplanes, people, kids, concessions! You have got to be kidding! An airshow is underway!? Like I don't have enough to manage! That explains the heavy traffic and constant chatter inbound. Get me out of here.*

I taxied back to runway five. I was number two for takeoff, after some sort of old-timey, open-cockpit biplane. A nice single-engine was behind me, and more airplanes behind the single-engine.

After a lengthy wait, I taxied onto the runway for takeoff.

Full power, manage pedals, rotate at 55 knots—I'm off. Climbing nice. Heading home. Finally, the airways are silent, peaceful. For the first time during the entire flight and for only a few moments I sat back in my seat, relaxed and let the tension melt away. I held the yoke with ease instead of the stranglehold that would suffocate a baby chick, scanned the instruments, and took a look outside. It all looked and felt familiar. Those inviting mountains, the safety of those valleys, that rich green late summer foliage, and the long stripes of flat farmlands along the North Carolina / Tennessee corridor below comforted me.

I contacted Tri-Cities (KTRI) approach, since I would be entering their TRSA (terminal radar service area) airspace. I knew the drill, but I was still tentative, and not 100 percent at ease with all of the communication terminology and procedures within controlled airspace. The approach controller recognized me from my earlier communication from 0A9 to Gatlinburg. That was reassuring, plus the guy was nice to me. He let me know that there was traffic at two o'clock and 4,000 feet. I didn't see it, but I let him know I was looking.

"Tri-Cities approach I have the Elizabethton airport in sight," I communicated to the nice traffic controller.

"4 Echo Quebec radar service terminated, good day," the nice traffic controller replied.

"4 Echo Quebec thank you. Good day," I replied with humble confidence and an unbelievable feeling in my heart and soul.

Winds are calm at 0A9. I'm going straight in runway six. Home FREE. I landed, bounced, added power, floated, landed, and cleared runway six.

I was all choked up. I could barely communicate. "Elizabethton traffic, 4 Echo Quebec clear of runway six," I transmitted, with a quiver in my voice.

I sat for a moment. *I did it, my first long cross-country solo. . . . And I NEVER EVER want to do it again.* My nerves were shot. I was mentally lifeless and physically exhausted from the self-induced tension.

Alex, the young, blond, and often serious lineman, directed me in and safely parked me. I shut down 4 Echo Quebec. He gave me a thumbs-up, chocked the airplane, asked if I needed anything, and then moved on to his next task.

Done. That's it. The long solo cross-country is under my belt. I still don't ever want to do it again.

I headed to the ground instruction room, recorded the trip in my log book and called Gunther. He was wicked excited and super proud. He told me that he and Olivia listened to me on www.liveatc.net and that I sounded professional and calm. I was glad to hear the joy in his voice.

One of my many training days at the Elizabethton Airport. Reliable EQ in the background.

I had been studying for the written exam for a couple of weeks. I read the entire written test guidebook and did 80 percent of the test questions contained therein. I called the test center at the Tri-Cities airport to schedule an appointment to take my private pilot's written exam.

Test day! *Had I really gotten to the point of taking the written exam for my private pilot's license?* It was all so surreal, like I was a windup toy and I hadn't run out of batteries yet, and my direction was purely mechanical. I was just going and going, without comprehension of what I was in fact doing. I wondered, *How in the world did I get here from being so afraid five months ago?*

I'm in the test center sitting in front of the computer screen. *"Click to begin your test."* Question one appears. I don't know the answer. My heart is beating fast. *Okay, take a deep breath, slow down, read the question, read the answers. Kim, you know this stuff.* My supportive, reasonable voice prevailed! *There are sixty questions, and two and a half hours to do this. Plenty of time.* Sooner rather than later, I settled in. The questions became familiar and the answers made sense. At least some of them did. I finished in an hour and a half.

In order to get my score, I had to click the Finish button. I couldn't do it. Anxiety and near hyperventilation had set in.

Seventy or better is passing. With fear, I clicked Finish. My breathing stopped. I closed my eyes and prayed to God that a seventy or better appeared. I opened my eyes and looked at the screen—*You have got to be kidding me!* A questionnaire stared me in the face! I answered the questionnaire with disgust and disdain, but also fairly and honestly. (Typically I skew questionnaires by answering them with sarcasm and cynicism just to prove that a face, a human body, real feedback is so much more valuable than a worthless piece of paper containing obscure and false data.)

Here we go again—click Finish. Same drill: pray to God, eyes closed. Open my eyes: *77. No way!* Life stopped.

I passed! The relief was so overwhelming that I almost collapsed. I was so happy . . . and scared to be proud for just a moment.

I left the room to get the test proctor so we could finish things up and I could leave. He wasn't immediately available, so I fetched my phone and purse. (They take that stuff away from you during testing.) I called Gunther, texted Krista, Sherri, Erich, Erich's wife Zoe, and John. Soon enough the test proctor finalized the test, gave me my score sheet, and I was outta there—on cloud nine.

As soon as I was in the solitude of my car, I called Mom and Dad; Mom wasn't home. But Dad just listened as I rambled on and on. Finally, when I gave him a minute to speak he said, "Wow! That's great, Kimmie!" in his heavy Austrian accent. That's all I let him say, before I started rambling again. Finally, I let him get off the phone, but not before saying, "Be sure to tell Mom, okay? Don't forget, tell Mom as soon as she gets home."

Gunther, Olivia, and I went away for the weekend to relax. They needed it as much as I did.

I was hoping to have my private pilot's license before winter set in. I flew nearly twenty hours over the next three and half weeks with and without John, practicing the final requirements in preparation for my oral and practical exam with the FAA examiner, Wayne. Many of the maneuvers weren't new, but certainly performing them convincingly in order to demonstrate that I had command of the airplane was a goal I needed to attain. Exercises like short and soft field landings, steep turns, all kinds of stalls, emergency landings, basic instrument flying, cross-country navigation, pilotage, dead reckoning, and night flying were some of the maneuvers I worked hard to perfect. Greasing a short field landing was rewarding, and realizing I could land an airplane safely without an engine was super-duper amazing.

The oral exam and check ride (practical exam) were all I had left to complete. Daniel, one of John's other students, who periodically patrols the state highways in Banner Elk and who had earned his private pilot's license not long before, stopped by my work office just before his shift one day to help me. He was dressed in full North Carolina State Trooper uniform—he even had his gun, handcuffs, and all that other stuff fastened securely around his waist. He spent about an hour with me going over *everything* Wayne had grilled him on during his oral exam, and each required maneuver he made him do on the check ride.

I took two pages of notes while Daniel racked his brain to ensure he communicated every detail I was expected to know. I studied those notes and my practical test guide thoroughly. Gunther quizzed me when he had the chance, and John texted me tons of questions. In the meantime, I completed the required four hours of practical test preparation with John and made several more solo flights before the check ride.

Late fall and winter were approaching fast. Acceptable weather days for a check ride were getting fewer as storms and wind were more frequent. The two-hour oral exam is typically followed by the check ride on the same day. Four, potentially five hours of being under the FAA microscope sounded like a lot to me.

I called the FAA examiner, Wayne, to schedule the oral exam and check ride. He was agreeable. We set the grueling day for Thursday, October 31. I drove to the Elizabethton airport early that morning. The weather was marginal. Nonetheless, I was determined to begin the final phase to earning my private pilot's license. Once I got to Elizabethton, I rechecked the AWOS (automated weather observation system). Ceiling and visibility were acceptable, but the forecast for wind shear was not in my wheelhouse. No one flies in wind shear conditions, not even forecasted wind shear conditions. Dan was at the Elizabethton airport, so I consulted him.

After reviewing the weather conditions once again, weighing all of the advice I had accumulated and considering my options, I decided not to fly that day. There was no way I was going to take on the possibility of wind shear conditions, an oral exam, and a check ride. The latter two were enough to contend with. Plus, the pilot is ALWAYS in command, therefore the final decision was mine to make.

I called Wayne. He agreed, no flying. But . . . we did arrange for the oral exam as soon as I could get to the Virginia Highlands airport by car, which was an hour later. We met in his small, windowless office.

I made it through two and half hours of airplane talk. Everything Daniel had briefed me about, Wayne threw at me. He asked me specifics, expected me to discuss concepts, explain and thoroughly demonstrate my understanding of a sectional chart, describe in detail my planned cross-country navigation log, and a few additional heavy concepts.

We began about eleven a.m. Around 1:15 p.m. I asked, "Can we be done now?"

He said, "Yes."

"Okay, well, how did I do?" I asked.

"You did very well," he replied.

"Yes," I whispered under my breath.

That evening, Olivia dressed up as Super Girl and we headed to Banner Elk's Halloween trunk-or-treat festivities. I didn't even have to dress up to feel like Supergirl.

Olivia and friends, Halloween 2013.

On Friday evening I called Wayne, who said the weather looked good for my check ride the next day. The weather looked perfect in the morning but was forecast to deteriorate after one p.m. My bag containing all the necessary items—headset, cross-country navigation log, sectional chart, E6B, personal back up notes, phone, extra sweatshirt, lunch, and snacks—was packed the night before. My night was restless. I woke up at six a.m. on Saturday, November 2, fidgety and nervous. It was still dark as I left the driveway at six thirty a.m. I drove to the Elizabethton Airport, flew 4 Echo Quebec to KVJI, and began my check ride at nine a.m.

It was cold, and rough weather was brewing. Systematically but carefully, I pre-flighted in the hangar to stay warm. When I finished, Jacob, another one of the Elizabethton Airport's line guys, moved the airplane outside onto the ramp.

4 Echo Quebec took me in like a familiar friend. The checklists were complete and by now the single engine was running. I placed the headset over my ears and flipped the master avionics switch on. There was no sound! I couldn't hear ATIS (automated terminal informational service: tells me which runway is active, some weather information, and other useful landing details and notices), AWOS, or me. I turned the avionics master switch off and then back on again, and troubleshot a while longer. With my cell phone I tried to call Gunther. He was out of range. I texted John. He offered some ideas, but couldn't help either.

Never ever have I flown without communication, especially solo. VFR (visual flight rules) doesn't require communication, but it's a really good idea and a safety measure that I personally rely upon. Still I took off for KVJI at 8:15 a.m. without radio communication, because I was getting there that morning to perform my check ride, no matter what! That much I knew. All was silent, except the drama in my head between my encouraging voice and my doubting one. The flight was smooth. I landed fine, parked just outside the terminal, and walked inside to find Wayne.

I found him instantly and told him about my dilemma. As we headed to the airplane, he said he would have a look, mentioned a few solutions I didn't understand, but also implied that we might not be able to perform my check ride. Devastation filled me up for a moment. Without missing a beat, I assured him that he could fix whatever was going on.

I did a stopover walk around before we both loaded into 4 Echo Quebec. After I turned the master power and the avionics switches on, Wayne fiddled with the audio panel and discovered that the radios were on com 1, while the switch was either on standby or com 2. Problem solved. He explained the problem and the solution, surprised that I hadn't figured it out on my own. I wanted to hug him anyway.

I taxied well under ten knots, nose wheel dead on the centerline, and performed my magneto check. Humble fear was inside me, but lately the frequency and repetition of training always backed me up, just like Dad had taught me all those years ago. During the preflight briefing, Wayne told me I was to fly my prepared cross-country route to the first checkpoint, which was five to seven minutes out. Takeoff was to be a short field. A short-field takeoff requires the shortest runway distance using wing flaps and full throttle.

I reached cruising altitude of 5,500 feet and stabilized the airplane. I viewed the ground for landmarks. He questioned me on a few: a railroad and Interstate 81. I identified the first check point: the intersection of Interstate 81 and the two-lane road to Damascus.

He instructed me to fly a 190-degree heading and descend to 4,500 feet. I did. Upon request, I performed a steep right-hand turn with no problems—but not before executing the required clearing turns first. Then I executed a power-on and -off stall. Stalls frighten me the most, but I kept it well hidden.

At 4,500 feet, Wayne noticed that there was a gap between the fuselage and my door. The door didn't appear to be shut all the way. He expressed grave concern. "We need to turn back, get on the ground immediately and shut the door properly!"

"No, no that's the way the door shuts all the time. It's secure. Don't worry. I won't fall out," I said. He took my word for it, but only after I twisted his arm. We continued the check ride.

I flew around a silo in the middle of a farm, but not very well. Then we moved over to his house, located on the banks of South Holston Lake, and he explained why a helicopter was sitting on the dock of his neighbor's house. (His neighbor uses it to go back and forth to work.) *Wow!* I thought while simultaneously executing the required maneuver flawlessly. I was to circle his house from above. Between checking my instruments, viewing the horizon, keeping an eye on his house to ensure I circled it properly, trying to locate the helicopter on the dock, physically flying the airplane, and showing interest in his helicopter story, I had performed that ground reference maneuver just fine.

Next, I placed the foggles on my head in preparation for the required instrument work. Foggles are glasses that restrict your vision so that all you can see is the instrument panel. I was restricted from seeing outside the airplane. Wayne gave me a heading, said to descend to a certain altitude while maintaining a specific airspeed, and keep the airplane level. I aced that. I took the foggles off and Wayne said, "Most students have trouble with steep turns and instrument work. You did both very well."

Yes!

We were just about finished with the check ride and out of

nowhere, Wayne suddenly took control of the airplane, jerking it to the right. Alarmed, he said, "Did you see that airplane?"

"No," I said calmly, but quickly scanned every window to see if I could tell what all the commotion was about. I felt like a well-trained fighter pilot. (Top Gun—you know!) "There it is!" I exclaimed. I saw it gracefully turning to the left in the opposite direction of our flight path, peacefully floating without a care in the world.

Whew, thank goodness. Alive one minute, dead the next. That's how fragile life is, I thought.

"It's a Saturday. Lots of weekenders are out for a joy ride," Wayne remarked with irritation. He told me to head back to KVJI and descend rather rapidly. I did.

When I have Gunther, John, or an FAA examiner with me, I can pretty much do whatever they tell me fairly well. It's the solo flying that challenges my confidence.

The weather was getting rough. The big change that time of year is wind. The little Skyhawk doesn't like strong winds, and neither do I. That's why when I smoothly touched down in ten knots crosswind gusting to fourteen on my check ride landing, I felt good. I must have passed. Then I carefully taxied my precious cargo, Wayne, back to the ramp.

"Did I pass?" I asked timidly.

"You did very well. Let's head inside and finish up the paperwork," Wayne said.

Yes. I was happy, very happy. The entire world along with its weight was off my shoulders.

I was supposed to get a picture of myself and the airplane for Krista (for Facebook I'm sure). But I didn't have time for that. Neither did Wayne. We went to his office and filled out the paperwork that he had to send to Federal Aviation headquarters in Oklahoma City for validation. He printed my temporary private pilot's license, and told me that if I don't receive the permanent one by February to give him a call. Oh yes, and he told me, "Congratulations!"

I texted everyone—"I'm a pilot."

CHAPTER ELEVEN
The Governor

"GUNTHER'S WAY" WASN'T ENOUGH

Gunther's Way wasn't enough. Expect to ride to Sugar's 5,300-foot peak in five minutes next season. The installation of a Doppelmayr high-speed, detachable, six-passenger chairlift will begin early this spring and is expected to be completed in time for opening day of the 2015-16 winter season. The existing Summit #1 lift will be refurbished and relocated to the bottom of Gunther's Way, providing access to the mountain's peak. Summit #2 lift will be shortened to the upper mid-point for beginners and/or an alternate access route to Sugar's north side, servicing Lower Flying Mile, Easy Street, Easy Street Extension, Gunther's Way, Little Nell, and Tiny Tim. The new lift system's architecture will streamline traffic flow and increase capacity by 2,000 people per hour.

—Sugar Mountain press release, April 2015

Over the following summer, a team of thirty-five Sugar Mountain Resort employees and a rotating crew from Doppelmayr worked and worked throughout the seven-month construction period.

Gunther and most of his Summit Express crew. Summer 2015. Front row: John Dearborn, Josh Clark, Vance Duggan, Derrick Peterson, Charlie Burleson, JC Steinbaugh, Nathan Hoilman, Steve Salmieri, Bill Burleson, Glenn Horney, Charlie Peters. Back row: Mike Singleton, Chase Martinson, Gunther, Chris Leonard.

The concrete company poured over thirty-nine foundations of assorted sizes and strengths. New lift station buildings were constructed and transported to the appropriate locations. In early August, twenty-one forty-foot shipping containers full of bull wheels, beams, and other drive and return terminal components came from Wolfurt, Austria. From mid-August through mid-September, ten tractor trailer trucks traveled from Salt Lake City and Canada to Sugar Mountain full of towers, wheels, and other shipments.

Gunther was at the center of it all mentally, intellectually, and physically. Every day, sometimes twelve hours a day, he drove the effort, coordinating the teams and the arrival of parts, checking and calculating the engineering, smoothing the bumps, monitoring the weather, handling the machinery, planning, staging and executing tasks, anything and everything to get the job done. His team was steadfast, dedicated, and hardworking. The project, though demanding, was energizing. Days were long, strenuous, tiring, overwhelming, fulfilling, worthwhile, and sometimes disappointing. Nights were short.

Parking lot #1 turns into the parts yard over the summer. Parts arriving from Salt Lake City, Canada, and Wolfurt, Austria.

Gunther and Doppelmayr's John Dearborn working the numbers.

I survived and even put in a half dozen or so manual labor work days myself! See that space-age station behind me in the picture to the right? Well, Freddie and I tightened the bolts that hold the skin, which protects the machinery inside. I was on a ladder, laid out on the dusty floor, squished under walking grates and under beams, on top of a crossbeam, and even pretzeled under the bull wheel, all to reach every bolt and ensure each one was tight. I smashed my head a few times, bumped my leg, bruised my shin, got a sore neck, and strained my arm muscles. And the guys ditched me for lunch. They just let me keep working. Didn't even bother to tell me it was lunch time. Pudge brought me a Coke from McDonald's, though.

Another day, John Dearborn and I screwed all sixty-eight metal number plates onto the lift chairs. John used the Dewalt drill and gave me an Allen wrench. Yup, that's right, an Allen wrench! It was 35 degrees Fahrenheit, the wind was blowing at 40 to 50 mph, and it was raining. I was dressed for the day's weather, but my chubby, small, fingers quickly became wet and numb. One of the chair's heavy steel footrests unexpectedly swung down, landing on my back and calf. Since a few of the guys were around I sucked up the urge to cry and later that night noticed two large bruises where I'd been hit. They were tender, black-blue-and-yellow, and decorated my body for a week.

On the job.

By the first of November, the installation of the Summit Express, the brand-new high-speed, detachable, six-passenger chairlift fitted to accommodate eight passenger gondolas, was complete. The new Little Gray chairlift, formerly known as the Summit #2 chairlift, had been shortened. It now ferries skiers and snowboarders to the top of the Easy Street Extension slope for beginners, and is an alternate access route for all guests providing access to the lower and north sides of the mountain. And the new GW chairlift, previously known as the Summit #1 chairlift, was refurbished and relocated to the bottom of the Gunther's Way slope. It transports passengers from the base of Gunther's Way to the mountain's peak.

The updated lift system's architecture streamlined traffic flow and increased the mountain's uphill transportation capacity to 10,520 people per hour. The project cost over five million dollars.

I had begun planning the Summit Express grand opening celebration back in May. You wouldn't believe the energy I expended. The guest list was an endless work-in-progress and included close to four hundred people: family, friends, local dignitaries and politicians, regional and state tourism representatives, local business owners, ski industry VIPs, the press, and project VIPs. In addition, we invited the public to attend the ribbon cutting and promised a complimentary ride on the Summit Express.

The invitations were designed, printed, and labeled by late September. I called or emailed many guests personally long before the formal invitations were sent. Since I didn't have a direct connection to the governor, the lieutenant governor, or any state-level politician, I began my research around June, and did what all regular citizens do—I googled them. Most websites

Come and see what we've built

When: Saturday, November 14, 2015 / 10:00am

Where: Sugar Mountain Ski Resort
1009 Sugar Mountain Drive
Village of Sugar Mountain, NC 28604

Please join us for the official grand opening of
Sugar Mountain Resort's Summit Express

Ride to Sugar's 5,300 foot peak in five minutes on our brand new Doppelmayr high speed, detachable, six passenger chairlift.
Brunch following the ceremony in the Last Run Lounge.

www.skisugar.com

led me down the following path—*Menu-> Contact-> Request an Engagement or Appearance-> Fill out an extensive online form.* Good grief! I filled out a few of those forms but it seemed useless and too much work; I concluded that they would only empty into a cyber pile of unattended requests. I had some connections through the North Carolina Division of Travel and Tourism, and Gunther had a business card from Lieutenant Governor Dan Forest, who'd stopped by Sugar Mountain Resort looking for a vote prior to his election in 2013. I exhausted all possible leads.

Lieutenant Governor Dan Forest's office provided event scheduling forms and contacts that seemed to be getting me somewhere. They included the press secretary's, director of operations', and assistant schedulers' email addresses for the lieutenant governor and the governor. That's all I needed, just a foot in the door. With academic diligence, I filled out every new required form. People with titles were answering me. Just not with the answers I wanted, nor in the time frame my impatience preferred. But I was communicating.

Time marched on.

On August 26 the governor's assistant scheduler contacted me.

Good morning Kim,

Thank you again for extending an invitation for Governor McCrory. Unfortunately, due to a prior commitment, he will be unable to attend. The Governor is honored to have been invited to attend.

Our office will notify you of any last minute changes to his schedule that would permit him to attend. I am currently working with the Department of Commerce to send a representative on behalf of the administration and will keep you updated.

Please do not hesitate to contact our office in the future with other events you would like the Governor to attend. Best wishes for a successful event.

Well, that's disappointing, I thought. *I'm still not giving up.*

In early October I sent via snail mail and email over four hundred invitations. Everyone who had already declined received a hard copy and an email invitation, regardless.

The lieutenant governor's press secretary and director of operations contacted me in early November.

I'm sorry for the delay, but we are figuring out our schedule still. As it looks right now, we are getting pulled to another event on behalf of the Governor on the other side of the state. With that being the case, I don't think we can get the LG to Sugar Mountain on 11/14.

My heart sank with disappointment. But for a millisecond I thought, *Kim, this means the governor is rearranging his schedule so he can come to Sugar Mountain. That's it, that's it! It's got to be the case.* When my optimism ceased, I went on with my workday, ultimately disappointed and not delusional about the reality of the governor coming to a tiny village in the western part of the state.

A few other close friends and colleagues had declined as well. "Gunther, it's useless. The governor's not coming. The lieutenant governor's not coming, the secretary of commerce isn't coming," I dragged on.

"Kim, we'll have a memorable celebration, no matter who comes," Gunther said.

But then a light bulb went off in Gunther's head. He decided he would call his friend and Village of Sugar Mountain resident Norman Cohen, who was well connected with, well . . . everyone from Margaret Thatcher to Ronald Reagan to Bill Clinton *and* the North Carolina governor. Norman was enthusiastic about his mission to recruit the governor and North Carolina Representative Craig Horn to the Summit Express celebration, and went to work.

"Norman will get it done, Kim," Gunther told me.

On November 3, an email from Norman advised me to email the event details to a specific address. I assumed it was one of the governor's key staffers. But maybe, it was directly to governor himself. I'll never know. Naturally, I dropped everything and sent the email promptly.

Over a week went by without any reply from the governor's office. My efforts in recruiting the rest of the four hundred invitees continued. The week of the event people came alive, excitement was brewing, RSVPs were rolling in, and the entire Sugar Mountain and Doppelmayr teams were planning, working, and executing like clockwork. We all functioned like an Olympic gold medal track and field relay team. But still no word from the governor.

Until . . . Norman forwarded me an email.

Norm—

The plan is for the governor to drive up and attend on Saturday.
I will send you our full briefing information we will need to ensure the governor, security and staff are fully prepared after I finish at this event I'm at now.

Thank you!
Director of Scheduling
Office of Governor Pat McCrory

Omigod, omigod, omigod! Breathe, Kim. No way. The governor's coming. Gunther! I have to tell Gunther. I stood up from my desk, sat down, stood up again, ran my hand through my hair, circled around for a moment and then dialed Gunther's cell phone number. I sat back down. *Answer the phone, answer the phone*, while I tapped my foot on the floor. Two rings later, which felt like an eternity, Gunther answered the chirping crickets ring tone he set specifically to indicate that his wife was on the other end.

"Hello," he said, somewhat perturbed.

"Holy cow, Gunther, Gunther, the governor's coming!"

"Okay, great, Kim. I'm upside down in a hole working on the lift. I gotta go now," he said.

What? "Do you realize what I just said?" I asked.

"Yes, Kim that's great. I knew you'd get it done."

"Okay, bye." I hung up.

Then the second email came less than two hours after the first, and forty-eight hours before the big event.

Norm/Kim—

Please see the attached form. We will need this completed to ensure the Governor, staff and security are fully prepared for the event. Let me know if you have any questions or concerns, please don't hesitate to contact me directly.

Thank you!
Director of Scheduling
Office of Governor Pat McCrory

The attached form was six pages long.

Two and a half hours and six pages later, I had completed

every question and sent it to the director of scheduling. That evening, I crafted a press release announcing the governor's and Mike Doppelmayr's expected attendance at Sugar Mountain Resort's Summit Express grand opening, and gave the news to our local county crier, Ken Ketchie, owner of *High Country Press*. At 8:45 the next morning, I received a phone call from the governor's western-region event coordinator. She informed me of the protocol, expected event-day procedures, and that the state police would be contacting our director of security shortly for a site visit. *Eeeech, this is serious,* I thought. Within a few hours a state trooper (not my friend, Daniel) had thoroughly inspected the Sugar Mountain Resort, in every place: even the bathroom in my office!

In between the phone call from the governor's western-region event coordinator and the state trooper's site visit, I remembered to broadcast the press release I had written late the night before.

Never give up.

On November 14, the grand opening ribbon cutting of the Summit Express was celebrated with our families, the local community, village, county, and state dignitaries, politicians including Governor Pat McCrory and North Carolina Representative Craig Horn, a group of Doppelmayr VIPs including owner Michael Doppelmayr and Doppelmayr USA president Mark Bee, and CWA (the Swiss gondola-maker owned by Doppelmayr) CEO Raimund Baumgartner. A few hundred snow sports enthusiasts cheered the ribbon cutting then filed aboard six-passenger chairs, complete with cushy seat features, spacious elbow room, and comfortable foot rests to Sugar's 5,300-foot peak in a mere five minutes.

Sugar Bear, Sweetie Bear, Gunther, Norman, the governor, me, and Mike Doppelmayr. See the governor's "detail" in the background?

The Governor, his "detail," Gunther, and I rode to the summit and back in the VIP gondola. I sat next to the governor.

Gunther, Governor McCrory, me, and the governor's detail in the VIP gondola on our way to the summit.

We talked about regular stuff. Well, regular stuff like skiing, the beautiful North Carolina mountains, the views we have of the Charlotte skyline and into Tennessee and Virginia from Sugar's peak, our investment, the new layout of the ski slopes, the plush, VIP gondola we were riding in, and the governor's first trip to Sugar when he was sixteen. He expressed the pleasure he experienced during his two-hour drive that morning from Charlotte via the windy, rural two-lane highway of NC-181 to Sugar Mountain, and was impressed with the engineering and flow of that mountain highway.

My angel (the one I saw in Austria when I was a little girl) was watching over Gunther and me that day. The El Niño weather pattern during the months of September, October, and November had produced 14.5, 7.9 and 8 inches of rain respectively. But on November 14 the sky was shiny blue, with temperatures in the 20s; the landscape was capped with the season's first man-made snow.

After the ribbon cutting and round-trip excursion on the Summit Express were complete, Gunther and I hosted 150 guests for brunch. Keith Lane, co-owner of Sugar's food service, went all out. The elaborate buffet included crab cakes, prime rib, baked turkey, fresh fruits, pastry items, veggies, and mimosas.

Gunther addressed the crowd. He was eloquent, and he held it together. In times past I would get nervous for him when he spoke in front of a crowd because he could get emotional, and an awkward silence would ensue. He would hold his breath, look away from the crowd, grimace, and fight with every bit of internal willpower to maintain a professional composure and not get all choked up. This time his composure was solid, proud. "When I first came to Sugar Mountain in 1976, there were three chairlifts and a rope tow. Today we have five chairlifts plus one of the most advanced detachable chairlifts in the country. The ski industry is an important part of the economy of the High

Country and we are glad to be a part of it. Snow sports affects everything from lodging, grocery stores, gas station, restaurants, and so much more. Our investment this summer has brought excitement throughout the High Country. Thank you to all of my staff, and especially to my wife, Kim, for making this come true. And now if I could ask the Honorable Pat McCrory, Governor of North Carolina, to say a few words."

Can you believe it? The governor of North Carolina came to our event!

During brunch, the governor spoke to the crowd about North Carolina's new branding, including a redesigned logo containing a mountain, the ocean and a new motto. "Our new state motto is 'North Carolina, Nothing Compares.' Nothing compares to North Carolina, and nothing compares to Sugar Mountain. Sugar Mountain Resort has been an icon in our state for years, attracting families from around the region and our country. This investment is a great sign for our economy and the confidence that businesses like Sugar Mountain Resort have in growing here," the governor said.

He was dynamic and energizing, rousing the crowd and inspiring patriotism. But a listener also. I sat next to him during brunch too. He asked where I had learned to ski. The conversation evolved into my ski racing career, my twin sister and her Olympic experiences, my husband, and flying. He asked which one of us was a better skier, Krista or me. That was a long answer as well. All he did was listen and ask inquisitive questions that required more listening on his part. Maybe I gabbed too much!

Pat McCrory had served a record fourteen years as the fifty-third mayor of Charlotte, but was now living in the governor's mansion in Raleigh and had spent some time in the governor's Western residence in Asheville. He liked our area, so I encouraged him and his "detail" to come back this winter to ski. Both said they would.

On Monday, November 16, two days after our magical day, a picture of the ribbon-cutting ceremony and an official release from the governor's press team was on the front page of www.governor.nc.gov and featured in the governor's November 16, 2015, NC Weekly Newsletter. And in late January he skied again on the slopes of Sugar Mountain.

How fantastic is that?

EPILOGUE

Not long ago, Gunther, Olivia, and I flew the Cheyenne to Beverly, Massachusetts, for one final getaway before the winter season began. I always fly right-seat in the Cheyenne now. I consider myself the copilot. The flight was ordinary until the Boston center traffic controller instructed us to turn left to a 340-degree heading. Then he told us to fly 190-degrees. Gunther and I looked at each other, puzzled. Still he followed the controller's instructions. Even more peculiar, next the controller commanded us to turn left to a 120-degree heading. Then circled us back to the original 60-degree vector.

"We just went in a circle," I said.

"Yup, that Boston center traffic controller just flew us in a circle," Gunther said.

We still haven't figured out why.

The next afternoon, the three of us watched the Boston Red Sox beat the New York Yankees in one of Derek Jeter's last games. Consumed by the infectious excitement, I became a half-crazed American sports fan: Cracker Jacks in hand, the winning team's ball cap on my head.

When I was representing my country competing as a member of the US Ski Team, I seldom experienced sports from the outside in, as a fan. I was always on the inside: the competitor, in the arena or on the training hill—focused with blinders on. Long gone are the days of competing on a world stage. Now, I was sitting a few rows from third base at Fenway Park, and I had the luxury and pleasure of being a fan. I felt and absorbed what it was like to root for a stranger, for a sport I wasn't passionate about, to be loyal to a team simply because I was native to the state it represented. I saw and experienced what accomplished athletes mean to regular people, how a professional sportsman's behavior and performance made me dream, hope that I could grow into more than I am now.

The trip to Fenway moved me.

It was moving for Gunther, too. Not an American native, but an American citizen since 1986, he clenched his fists together when the Red Sox (of course he has to be a Red Sox fan) made a good play or ran someone home. He ate peanuts and got all choked up when the national anthem was played.

"Don't ever forget you're an Austrian," his mother reminds him. He doesn't, but he's grateful, proud, and honored to be an American.

"Many people live in a free society, governed by democracy, but only Americans know how to handle freedom. It's unique and special to be American, to be born here, to be a product of the American society. Freedom isn't free. You have to work at it and for it. Americans respect freedom. They are a disciplined, compassionate, hard-working, and giving society," Gunther often tells me, or anyone else who will listen.

The next morning I woke to one, loud, squawking sea gull. I pulled the drapes back to see the beautiful blue sky and the sunshine of a new day through the skyscrapers on a Sunday morning from the eleventh floor, in a corner room of the opulent Boston Harbor Hotel. I got dressed, took the elevator to the lobby, exited through the harbor-side door, took a morning stroll along Rowe's Wharf, and meandered back under the hotel's magnificent archway.

View from Boston Harbor Hotel, with seagull, 2014.

Years ago, Krista and I had ventured by water taxi from Boston's Logan airport to Faneuil Hall Marketplace for some carry-on reminders of home before we boarded an airplane headed to Europe for a lengthy competition season. The water taxi had dropped us off at Rowe's Wharf, directly in front of this very hotel. I loved smelling the ocean air and hearing the seagulls while strolling under the Hotel's archway and along the wharf's neatly kept waterfront. Back then, I daydreamed about staying in that hotel, just once. Remember?

Two and a half decades later, Gunther, Olivia and I had driven up to the front entrance, where the valet politely welcomed us, tagged and managed our luggage, then escorted us to the check-in desk. We walked through the rotating doorway where guests rustled about the five-star hotel, as if living in this type of elegance and grace was normal. I looked around, taking in everything from the oversized vase of sunflowers on the round table to the beautiful décor that made me feel like John Adams might be lurking nearby. I enjoyed the expansive views of Boston Harbor complete with a nest of sailboats just beyond the extravagant yachts tied to the dock.

It was enchanting, everything I had imagined.

Maybe that Boston air traffic controller had been trying to tell us something, or maybe it was my angel watching over me, but there was no question in my mind that on that day, I had come full circle.

ACKNOWLEDGMENTS

When words flowed onto the paper I began to reveal myself. The joy of writing metamorphosed into the shape of a memoir. Then came editing. Simple words developed into more definitive, sophisticated ones, or were deleted all together. Rearranging and sequencing turned into a game of Twister. When fact-checking agreed with my memory, I was happy. Expanding or elaborating on seemingly incomplete passages to enrich the reader's experience became obvious. And so went the technical process of writing my memoir.

Along the way, I invited a few trusted or objective souls to read over the voluminous words that filled the once-empty space. Betsy Thorpe, Maya Myers, and Diana Wade were the professionals I relied upon. Of course each family member took a trip down memory lane, whether they wanted to or not. Olivia and a few friends, like Diane Wilcox and Sally Utter, offered useful feedback that sent me editing the manuscript *again*. Then there were those who never read a word, but influenced me nonetheless.

Thank you.

Reassurance to publish *Fly Baby: The Story of an American Girl* came from random and unexpected family, friends, acquaintances, colleagues, and strangers who reached out to tell me how my first published book, *The Aviatrix: Fly Like a Girl*, moved them. Some even took on the challenge of flying or picked it up again.

And my deepest gratitude goes to the wholesale buyers of

The Aviatrix, who took a gamble on an unproven new author. They are: Fred and Margie Pfohl of Fred's General Mercantile, Mike Mola of Diamond Creek Resort, Toni Littleton of the Elk River Club, Bill Pillows of the Appalachian State University Bookstore, Dan Cogan of the Elizabethton Municipal Airport, Janette Barber of Aircraft Spruce, Pam Phillips of Tri-City Aviation, Heather Ward of Lees McRae College bookstore, Jesse Pope of Grandfather Mountain Nature Museum & Gift Shop, Tina Houston of Reid's Café, Jeff Shuttle of Lowes Foods, Thea Young of Footsloggers, Nicole Lawry of Barnes & Noble Asheville Mall, Vicki Combs and Robert Nobles of Barnes & Noble Johnson City, Katherine Weathers of Barnes & Noble Buckhead, Atlanta, Daniel Gainey and Julie Jones of Barnes & Noble Biltmore Park at Town Square.

CPSIA information can be obtained
at www.ICGtesting.com
Printed in the USA
FFOW05n2305210117

9 780997 150711